A.J,

First reading for

"Artois"

Love

Dad.

EXECUTE...
or
BE EXECUTED

EXECUTE...
or
BE EXECUTED

EIGHTEEN WAYS TO MOVE
STRATEGIC THINKING
TO STRATEGIC DOING

SAM GEIST

ADDINGTON &
WENTWORTH
INC.

Toronto, Ontario, Canada
Naples, Florida, United States

Published simultaneously in Canada and in the United States
by Addington & Wentworth, Inc.

> For information address:
> Addington & Wentworth, Inc.
> 327 Renfrew Drive, Suite 301
> Markham, ON CANADA L3R 9S8
> (905) 475-1022

First Edition
First Printing

Library and Archives Canada Cataloguing in Publication

Geist, Sam, 1945-
"EXECUTE... OR BE EXECUTED": eighteen ways to move strategic
thinking to strategic doing

ISBN 13: 978-1-896984-13-1
ISBN 10:   1-896984-13-4

Includes index
1. Management. 2. Strategic planning. 3. Organizational change.
4. Organizational effectiveness. I. Title.
HD31.G35 2008   658.4   C2007-907231-3

Dedication

To business men and women everywhere
who recognize all the possibilities around them
—and work every day to turn those possibilities
into reality.

ACKNOWLEDGMENTS

It is with much appreciation and sincere gratitude that I would like to thank the following for their skills—their encouragement—and their outstanding execution of the myriad of requests I put before them.

To all the manuscript readers who so generously gave hours of their time to provide me with insightful suggestions and observations—Sherry Abbott, Dan Butler, Luther Carlson, Denny Clements, Mark Cywilko, Mark Derry, Pat Dunne, Bruce Engelhardt, Ron Funk, Michael Geist, Aaron Geist, Joshua Geist, Val Halamandaris, Joe Jankoski, Ismail Merchant, Margaret Keane, Harry Rhoads, Charles Schade, Jacobo Schatz, Steven Simms, Keith Talbot, Debbie Vaillancourt, Gary Welch.

To Fortunato Aglialoro for his expert design and meticulous attention to detail.

To Pat Kennedy for her thorough editing and helpful perspective.

To Michelle Avoledo for her invaluable assistance from start to finish—no job was too small or too large to be tackled professionally.

To my family—children Michael & Allison, Aaron & Sara, Rebecca & Jacobo and Josh & Liane, and grandchildren, Jordon, Ethan, Gabrielle, Mimi, Ilana, Shoshi, Yoni, Orly, Tamar, Samantha and Chloe for their love, ongoing support and interest, and giving me lots to smile about.

And finally to my wife, Rene for standing by my side every step of the way—throughout this project and all the other projects we have undertaken together.

Sam Geist, *2008*

TABLE OF CONTENTS

INTRODUCTION

THE NAME OF THE GAME IS "EXECUTE... OR BE EXECUTED"

What I now know _____

Execution is not part of the strategy. Execution IS the strategy.

> "**execution** (ek-si-kyu-shun) n **1:** taking action. **2:** the act of performing, of implementing. **3:** doing what is required to give validity to an idea, a plan, a strategy."

Contrary to popular opinion, it's not strategy alone that determines business success. It's how well you implement that strategy, how well you execute those ideas and plans. A failure to execute is fatal. Execute... or be executed.

To celebrate its tenth anniversary, *strategy + business* magazine asked readers and business writers alike what was most likely to affect the way businesses are conducted in the long run. Just over 49% of those who voted chose "execution." (Execution trumped "a learning organization" (46.6%); "corporate values" (40.1%) and "customer relationship management" (40.1%)—the next three on the list.)

> *"I didn't get where I am by thinking about it or dreaming about it. I got there by doing it."*
>
> **—Estée Lauder** (1908-2004), co-founder, Estée Lauder Companies

EXECUTION IS CRITICAL!

Effective execution requires looking at your entire business and finding ways to improve each part of the process—your leadership, your people, your business process, your partners, your technological skill. It requires really implementing the improvements you see necessary, getting your employees to fully participate, measuring your progress, adjusting, correcting, applauding, and then repeating the process all again… and again… and again.

At a recent Society for Information Management (SIM) conference, the question was raised, "What keeps CEOs awake at night?" The Conference Board findings, presented by UNISYS indicates that the #1 concern of 38.3% of respondents, the one that keeps them awake at night, is excellence in execution; their #3 concern according to 31.8% of respondents is consistent execution of strategy by top management.

The power of execution is not new—not revolutionary. For years, "business gurus" have touted the importance of real execution. Despite all their rhetoric, the majority of organizations continue to do as they have always done. Execute too little, too late. They watch good strategies, great ideas and innovative plans languish and eventually disintegrate, as they sit idly by and wonder what happened.

> *"After all is said and done, there is far more said than done."*
>
> —Belasco & Stayer,
> authors of *Flight of the Buffalo*

Why is Wal-Mart so dominant? Why is Southwest Airlines so successful? Why is Rooms-to-Go so popular? Why is McDonald's doing so well? Why is Starbucks expanding so quickly?

They execute! The winners always out-execute the laggards.

> *"Knowing is not enough; we must apply. Willing is not enough; we must do."*
>
> —Johann Goethe (1749-1832)

With the value of execution so apparent, why don't more organizations get on the bandwagon? Why don't more leaders lead the charge to execute? Why don't more employees follow their leaders? Why don't more organizations develop do-able processes to execute?

What thwarts execution? Many organizations on the cusp of executing, get bogged down in its challenging demands. They find the road to successful execution is often under construction. There are delays, roadblocks, unforeseen problems. They don't know where to begin. The signposts along the way are confusing. It's easy to get lost. It's much easier to stay where they are and just talk about their strategies and ideas and plans.

EXECUTION IN ACTION

Those who execute, triumph. Meet Sandra Wilson, founder of Robeez Footwear Ltd. When she became frustrated that she couldn't find a pair of soft-soled shoes for her 18-month-old toddler's chubby feet, she took action.

"Talk does not cook rice."

—Chinese proverb

She designed her own shoes, cutting up an old leather purse for material. When she was satisfied with her creation, she took the first steps to make it happen. She took 20 pairs to a gift show. Sales now top $15 million in more than 30 countries, and Robeez has just been sold to Stride Rite for $30.5 million.

Those that execute grow. Those that are already big, execute to stay big. In his book, *Good to Great*, Jim Collins analyzed the characteristics of companies that according to his criteria had become great. He discussed what enabled them to make the leap from good to great—what empowered them to pass their competitors. Among all the other qualities for greatness, each of these eleven companies executed—day-by-day—step-by-step—action-by-action. (Much like Sandra Wilson—but on a grander scale). They transformed themselves slowly into what they needed to become in order to succeed. During interviews, they all claimed that there was no sudden flash of realization—no miracle moment. By executing their strategies they found that they had evolved into exceptional companies.

6.2

When I speak to or facilitate for various groups at conferences or meetings, I always discuss the significance of execution with them. I take it even one step further. During the session I distribute cards and ask participants (anonymously of course) to rate their company's execution from poor to excellent on a scale from one to 10. Because no one will be able to identify anyone's particular score, I assume they are being honest with me.

How would you rate your company?
What do you think is the average score?

It's 6.2. And in today's marketplace, 6.2 doesn't cut it. That's why I wrote this book.

"There's a way to do it better—find it."

—**Thomas Edison** (1847-1931), inventor

When I point out to participants that a rating of 6.2 is abysmal, they agree. However, everyone has reasons or excuses. Let's look at some of them and then let's focus on getting rid of the roadblocks in order to put together a clear and effective roadmap for successful execution.

EIGHT REASONS EXECUTION IS SO POOR

1. There's lots of discussion on what needs to be done, but very little clear, detailed communication on how to do it.

2. The common (and mistaken) belief of those at the top of an organization that it is the responsibility of the managers, the bosses, to come up with the plan and the strategies and then hand over those plans, strategies, ideas, to the "common folk" down below whose responsibility it is to implement them. (I have on more than one occasion heard it said from the corner office, "I don't do grunt work.")

3. There's lack of training, so those who are "to execute" aren't sure what is expected of them or don't know specifically how to do it.

4. There's lack of realization that the planning process and the execution process are not independent of each other. They are connected from start to end.

5. There's lack of patience. Execution takes a long time, much longer than planning. It is a step-by-step process that must be organized and measured on an on-going basis. It's not a one-shot deal.

6. There's too little understanding that engaging, energizing, and rewarding staff is a vital and constant component of execution.

7. Too many fail to take advantage of all the internal and external resources available for the duration of the execution process.

8. Many fail to realize the role technology plays in today's marketplace. They don't utilize IT effectively.

Those organizations that can find their way to raising the 6.2 average have much to gain. What can you do—your organization do to improve your rating by one point?

One morning, not long ago, while I was on a stopover in Atlanta, I went into the lounge to work until it was time to board my plane for the final leg of my trip home. As I sat there, I overheard a conversation among three Wal-Mart executives and their new hire, who (it appeared) they were taking to a regional meeting. He was gushing about how happy he was to be working at Wal-Mart and how great a company it was. He then asked the three execs, "How do you do it? How do you stay ahead of everybody else?" One of them replied, "It's no big deal, we just out-execute them."

"High expectations are the key to everything."

—**Sam Walton** (1918-1992), founder of Wal-Mart and Sam's Club

It's time to learn a lesson from organizations that execute. They realize that moving strategy from innovation and planning to reality means everyone in the entire organization must be in it together, on the same page, moving forward. Talk is, after all, only talk. Without execution, all your great plans and strategies and ideas are merely dreams.

"You can either take action or you can hang back and hope for a miracle. Miracles are great but they are so unpredictable."

—**Peter F. Drucker** (1909-2005), writer, management consultant and university professor

This book will help you, your organization, and your people to use the organizational tools you already own to close the gap between your dreams and reality. After one of my speaking engagements, a participant came up to me and said, "Now I know why I have a flat forehead. It's from repeatedly hitting myself on the forehead, with my palm, while repeating, 'This is not rocket-science. Why didn't I think of that?'"

This book is filled with "why didn't I think of that?" ideas. It will assist you to look outside your traditional viewing (and thinking) platform. (Research has shown that 90% of what we learn comes from outside our business.)

Research information and examples abound. Use them not only to consider changing your modus operandi, use them to help you decide *how to* change your approach.

Keep in mind that execution is not a simple, one-step, one-time task. Execution is touched by so many factors, from the style of the leader, to the mindset of the people—from the skills brought to the table to the environment in which execution is to take place—from the partners involved to the technology utilized—and much, much more. Each part of the book focuses on one area of execution. Each chapter within that part concentrates on one important aspect of that area—and is written to be quite complete on its own. Read the chapters in the order that they are written, or feel free to read just those that are most relevant to your situation.

At the conclusion of each part I've included Marketplace Lessons that I've learned along the way. I share them in my weekly *QuickBites* e-newsletter and find that they offer up valuable learning experiences.

After you have read the book, choose the chapter(s) that you feel are most useful to your people and pass the book on to them.

All together the book discusses valuable elements of execution and offers many invaluable suggestions you will use on an ongoing basis. These will assist you to move from strategic thinking to strategic doing. Take charge of execution! Execute… or Be Executed.

PART I:
EXECUTION STARTS HERE

Chapter One: THE GAP—CLOSE IT

What I now know _____

The disconnect between knowing and doing, between ideas and implementation—between plans and execution, must be eliminated.

A huge amount of time, money, and resources is invested annually by organizations in order to come up with "the big strategy" that will magically transform them from frumpy to fabulous. Unfortunately it just doesn't work that way. If only an equivalent amount of time, money and resources was invested by these very organizations to execute their plan. Then it would happen.

A 2006 study by Connecticut-based On Point Consulting found that almost half (49%) of the leaders surveyed, agreed that there was a gap between their strategies and their execution and of these, 64% weren't fully confident that their companies would actually be able to close that gap. Bain & Company research corroborates these findings. Clearly a critical gap exists between the strategic plans developed in an organization and their implementation— and this gap must be closed in order to achieve long-term marketplace success.

"Strategy gets you on the playing field, but execution pays the bills."

—**Gordon E. Eubanks, Jr.**, former President and CEO, Symantec Corporation

"82% of Fortune 500 CEOs surveyed indicated that they feel their organization did an effective job of strategic planning. Only 14% of the same CEOs indicated that their organization did an effective job of implementing the strategy."

—*Forbes* magazine

"Corporate strategies are intellectually simple; their execution is not. The question is, can you execute? That's what differentiates one company from another."

—**Larry Bossidy**, author and former CEO, Allied Signal and Honeywell

ELIMINATE THE STRATEGY-EXECUTION GAP

Determine the root cause of the disconnect between strategy and performance in your organization. While most organizations have the strategy, they lack an actual strategy-execution process. Some organizations cannot articulate their strategy in a clear, simple, consistent voice—a requirement for enabling discussion and encouraging followership. Others own poor, vague or unworkable strategies that are simply impossible to implement.

Involve your people in the planning process, since they'll be the ones involved in the implementation process. After outlining your strategy to them, give them the opportunity to help develop the steps to build the bridge between strategy and implementation.

Sadly, many employees don't understand the corporate aims of their organization, let alone see themselves as an integral part of the solution. Harvard Business School findings suggest that 95% of employees do not understand their organization's strategy. Do your employees understand?

All employees must know what they are doing, why they are doing it and be fully committed to doing what they are doing. A well-known story illustrates this. A group of U.S. senators were visiting NASA at a time when funding was being threatened. One senator asked a man cleaning the floor, "So, what are you doing here?" The man answered, "I'm here putting a man on the moon!"

Ask yourself some illuminating questions.
- ❖ How closely do your employees identify and associate their own roles with your organizational goals?
- ❖ How accurately are they able to measure their performance?
- ❖ Do they understand what resources are at their disposal?
- ❖ Do they know how to access them effectively?
- ❖ Do they get the tools, training, and support they need to continue to be valuable employees while their jobs evolve?

MAKE IT HAPPEN

Link your strategic priorities to budget, so funding and resources can be appropriately allocated. (HBS studies show that 60% of typical organizations don't do this.)

Link your strategic plans to your organizational structure, otherwise the strategies will be ignored.

Link your strategic plans to accepted guidelines or models to facilitate implementation.

> *"I believe every CEO should walk up to the head of human resources and ask two questions: one, do we have the skills, top to bottom, in every job, in every country to execute our strategy; and two, where there is a gap, where are we investing our development money and what kind of return are we getting from that investment?"*
>
> **—Susan Bowick,**
> retired Hewlett-Packard veteran

OFFICE OF STRATEGY MANAGEMENT

Some organizations have created an Office of Strategy Management (OSM) at their corporate levels to eliminate the disconnect between strategy and execution. The role of the OSM is to oversee strategy-related activities, keeping everyone on the same page—from inception to completion. The person in this position facilitates, coaches, and co-ordinates the process (rather than providing hands-on execution), so that strategic implementation is enabled throughout the organization.

As reported in *American Executive* magazine, organizations that successfully create and utilize an OSM, experience measurable results. For instance when Chrysler Group instituted an OSM, it generated $1.2 billion in earnings and launched a new series of cars in 2004, while the rest of the U.S. auto market fizzled.

EMBRACE TRANSPARENCY WITHIN YOUR ORGANIZATION

Secrets are problematic. They're counterproductive in today's marketplace. Sharing information with employees enables them to be innovative, to use their best judgment, and to respond to customers' needs. In fact, in the On Point Consulting survey, just mentioned, 64% of respondents said that open and honest communication from leaders (even when they don't have all the answers) would make executing easier during changing times. Richard Lepsinger, president of On Point advises leaders to engage in "change talk," asking employees questions like "What is your perspective of the importance of the change/situation?" in order to keep lines of communication open.

"In most companies, management controls information and therefore controls people. By sharing information, we stay aligned to the vision of a shared fate."

—John Mackey,
CEO, Whole Foods Market

Transparency also turns scrutiny—once the monopoly of management—on its ear. Employees in the lower echelons need to see clearly what management is doing and why. Management must not only be prepared to explain their actions, they must also behave consistently in accordance with the values advocated by the organization. Employees who are in the know have little leniency for a double-standard.

Whole Foods Market moved transparency to an "open book" philosophy, sharing with staff all financial information, from salaries to profitability, believing that fully informed employees make smarter decisions. It seems to be working as they continue to execute openly.

During a difficult financial time for SAS (Scandanavian Airlines), the CEO gave his employees the choice between layoffs or huge customer-service improvements together with across-the-board pay cuts, in order to regain profitability. They chose the latter. By sharing his problem, he galvanized his organization, earning trust and commitment from employees and increased customer and shareholder support as well.

SUSTAIN EMPLOYEE SUPPORT AND COMMITMENT

Leaders realize that if they don't get employees committed to the strategy, it won't happen, and many do a good job on the initial sell to their staff. But after a couple of months, employee commitment and support trails off. It is at this point that successful organizations take action to get back on track. The same On Point Survey indicates that, if an organization doesn't take corrective action quickly (in a month or three) there is little likelihood that it will be able to achieve its objectives.

To keep employees' commitment and enthusiasm from flagging, celebrate each success along the way. To keep the plan from fading, stay involved every step of the way. On Point's, Lepsinger advises that you "treat your plan as a living document—one that you keep coming back to and revising as you learn and discover unanticipated problems and opportunities."

Toyota has been steadily moving forward for years thanks to its *kaizen*, Japanese for "continuous improvement." At Toyota they revisit their strategy, looking for holes, and then plug them. They diligently study problems, and then they solve them. They execute. They've raised the bar for the whole industry.

SIX SIMPLE RULES TO CLOSE THE GAP

1. Find the root cause of the gap.

2. Connect strategies and plans with actions and priorities.

3. Speak the same language throughout the organization.

4. Monitor performance.

5. Identify and remove execution problems.

6. Focus on improving capabilities.

Closing the strategy-execution gap becomes easier when everyone in your organization gets together and gives a little push.

Keeping the strategy-execution gap closed is critical to the growth and prosperity of your organization. The only way to do that—is to execute... execute... execute.

RATE YOURSELF

☐ On a scale of 1 to 10: How big is the gap between strategy and execution in my organization?

What steps can be taken to close the gap by one point?

_____

_____

_____

_____

THE BOTTOM LINE

To close the strategy-execution gap for long term success, takes on-going discipline—day in and day out.

Chapter Two: THE FACE OF THE ORGANIZATION

What I now know _____

High-performance organizations continue to execute their strategy while they change and evolve.

There has been a fundamental shift in today's business model. Expectations have changed. Expectations of those who work in today's workplace have changed. Expectations of investors and observers and customers of today's companies have changed. The concept of value—how it is created and what it represents—has changed.

> _"Start earlier. Think smarter. Act faster."_
>
> —**Smith Barney,** financial advisors

The mandate of high-performance organizations, in today's business environment is to evolve in sync with this shift by constantly focusing on ways to improve and innovate and always be looking for ways to meet new expectations. In order to accomplish this—in order to stay ahead of the competition, they must keep executing their strategy _at every level_ in their company.

It can be done. How is your business executing its strategy and changing and evolving at the same time? Look at your business and compare its processes with these five ways high-performance organizations execute.

FIVE WAYS HIGH-PERFORMANCE ORGANIZATIONS EXECUTE

1. High-performance organizations employ people who think and act.

They operate in the unrelenting pursuit of improvement and innovation. They are proactive. They innovate, create, move

> _"Companies that want to create tomorrow's breakthrough ideas will have to find ways to break down the barriers between departments, fields and cultures and encourage their people to pursue different ideas and connect with diverse networks of people."_
>
> —**Frans Johansson,** author, Managing Director, Medici Capital Management

forward, execute the plan. They align themselves closely—very closely with their customers. They test every goal and activity against how well it anticipates, meets, and exceeds customer wants and needs.

Google requires its employees to dedicate 20% of their time to their own personal projects: ideas that don't fit neatly into Google's established plan. Google has kept track of these projects and has found that virtually all of their new product ideas come from the time that employees have spent working on their own projects.

2. High-performance organizations achieve extraordinary levels of productivity through training, developing, leading, and engaging their people.

They close the gap between knowing and doing, they eliminate the disconnect that occurs in so many organizations by training and developing their people. The expertise of their people allows them to raise the bar and enables them to see marketplace opportunities with a new perspective. They are always continuing to look for new ways to increase their productivity. They are always searching for and finding new ways to lead and engage their people. They are forever executing.

Toyota provides an excellent example of world-class speed, flexibility, innovation, and implementation. CEO Fujio Cho's fear that "there's always tremendous danger that if we relax, even for a moment, we could lose momentum and be thrown to the bottom," drives the company to lead and engage their people straight past the competition. He is working to shorten the chain of command, improve accountability, and speed-up the decision-making process. He wants a structure in place that instantly responds, so "if there's a problem, I want to hear about it in an hour." Towards that goal, Toyota plants have "pull cords" on their assembly lines. Should anyone at any time see a problem, they have the power to stop the line. Everyone is charged with the responsibility to look for and to correct deficiencies. At the same time, employees are given cash rewards for ferreting out glitches in production and devising solutions for them.

To improve the quality of management candidates and therefore execution, Toyota recently established the Toyota Institute, an in-house leadership-development program run in partnership with the Wharton School of Business.

3. High-performance organizations regard information technology as both a vehicle for implementing operational excellence and providing a competitive advantage.

This perspective enables them to catapult ahead of their competition.

By guaranteeing time-definite arrival of goods, utilizing an absolutely, positively reliable delivery system and by reinforcing that operational mandate with a technologically advanced system, FedEx and UPS have both successfully benefited their customers by enabling them to use just-in-time inventory control—a productivity linchpin of the new economy. FedEx and UPS now control so much more than simple on-time delivery. They provide their customers with access to a growing global marketplace through a network of supply-chain transportation businesses and related information services. Their reliability and long reach are helping businesses who use them to become more efficient—and in the process FedEx and UPS have become verbs.

4. High-performance organizations live and breathe long-term sustainability.

Their raison d'être is to maximize value for the benefit of all stakeholders—employees, customers, and investors. Starbucks has created a worldwide empire based on the notion that everyone wants to feel that they're important and they deserve to indulge in a pleasurable experience. Starbucks has gone even further with its special coffee cards

"Price is price. Value is the total experience."
—Sam Geist

and secret language. (My daughter steps up happily and orders "a grande, decaf, soy latte, extra hot, no foam, fill it up" for $$.) Making people feel good and warm and a member of an elite club is an excellent strategy for sustainability. What is your strategy for sustainability?

While traveling in Shanghai, China, we ventured into an old marketplace. A Starbucks stood next door to a dim sum restaurant where everyone was washing down their dim sum lunch with a cup of Starbucks coffee. The company's international strategy, so well executed, has happily joined east and west.

"Execution gives us the license to expand the brand."

—**Howard Schultz**, Chairman and Chief Global Strategist, Starbucks Corporation

According to *Fortune* magazine, Starbucks remains one of America's most admired companies. Its mission highlights its guiding principles and creates a benchmark with which to measure the validity of its decisions and to execute those decisions.

STARBUCKS MISSION

▼ Provide a great work environment and treat each other with respect and dignity.

▼ Embrace diversity as an essential component in the way we do business.

▼ Apply the highest standards of excellence to the purchasing, roasting and fresh delivery of our coffee.

▼ Develop enthusiastically-satisfied customers all the time.

▼ Contribute positively to our communication and our environment.

▼ Recognize that profitability is essential to our future business.

5. High-performance organizations find new ways to innovate.

They're always changing, moving, imple-menting. Apple may not be using a traditional strategy—*Time* magazine called it "an odd company," but it certainly keeps the marketplace buzzing. While most high-

"Discovery consists of seeing what everybody has seen and thinking what nobody has thought."

—**Albert von Szent-Gyorgy** (1893-1986), American biochemist and 1937 Nobel prize winner

tech firms focus on one or two sectors, Apple does them all at once. It makes its own hardware, its own operating system (to run on that hard-ware), and its own software (to run on that operating system).

Apple also makes electronic devices that expand and connect to its users' capabilities. The iPhone, the latest in its iPod family, has revolution-ized the mobile phone industry. Not only that, it is the first truly portable mobile computer. Apple also runs online services that furnish content to these devices as well as being in the retail business with brick-and-mortar Apple stores. The company's diversity is mind-boggling, as is the speed and the "marketplace accuracy" of its innovation and execution.

If you study high-performance companies, one very important com-mon attribute surfaces. That is their ability to consistently innovate to deliver results—their ability to execute their strategy. It's that simple and that difficult.

—— ✳ ✳ ✳ ——

RATE YOURSELF

☐   On a scale of 1 to 10: How good is my organization at growing, innovating and executing hard-to-replicate capabilities?

What does it need to do to improve by one point?

_____

_____

_____

_____

THE BOTTOM LINE

High-performance is not an end goal, it is a continuous journey that requires understanding your customers well, searching for innovations, finding the means to keep your people engaged, and executing your strategies consistently.

Chapter Three: THE FACE OF THE LEADER

What I now know _____

Leadership is a verb.

Leaders must lead. They must scrutinize, demand, push, involve, and ramp up their skills and talents and the skills and talents of those around them. They must execute the plan! In our tumultuous business environment it is tough to be a really good leader—expectations run so high—challenges are so risky.

On what all successful leaders share:

"Courage. You are trying to engender a passion and a desire to do something new. And new is scary. As a leader, you are putting your ass on the line to make it happen. So you should be scared."

—Kevin Sharer, CEO, Amgen

SEVEN LEADER "MUST-HAVES" IN ORDER TO EXECUTE

After speaking to a great many leaders and analyzing a glut of research, I've refined a leader's "must-haves-to-make-it-happen" to the following seven requisites:

1. Know Yourself

Today's leaders must clearly recognize their strengths and weaknesses. Doing this affects strategy, affects execution, affects productivity, and affects profitability. By recognizing (and maximizing) their strong suits, by accepting (and minimizing) their weaknesses and by utilizing the complementary skills of their employees, they are able to take advantage of marketplace opportunities and grow the company.

"Never hire or promote in your own image. It is foolish to replicate your strength and idiotic to replace your weakness. It is essential to employ, trust, and reward those whose perspective, ability, and judgment are radically different from yours. It is also rare, for it requires uncommon humility, tolerance and wisdom."

—Dee W. Hock, founder of Visa International/*Fast Company*

Fred Smith, CEO of FedEx, is aware that in today's marketplace it is now impossible for the head of a company to know everything. While he can look over accounting functions and understand the fundamentals of information technology, Smith is not formally trained in these fields. He needs his peoples' expertise to help him grow his company.

2. Identify Business Opportunities

Successful leaders maintain a real understanding of their business and its environment. They can identify opportunities, "holes" in the marketplace and then go about filling them. CEMEX, founded in Mexico in 1906, grew from a small regional cement firm into a huge global building-solutions company by changing the existing model of the business under the leadership of CEO Lorenzo Zambrano, (grandson of the founder). CEMEX provides its customers with the most efficient and effective solutions—just-in-time cement and ready-mix concrete—where it is needed, when it is needed. In the process Zambrano with his managerial excellence, has raised its profitability many times over. CEMEX creates enviable opportunities for itself by executing the real purpose of its business and by focusing on continuously improving for the benefit of its customers.

3. Give Your People What They Need

No leader runs alone. Joseph Rost of the University of San Diego in his book, *Leadership for the Twenty-first Century*, defined leadership as "an influence relationship among leaders and followers who intend real changes that reflect their mutual purposes. The key is that the most wanted changes must not only reflect the wishes of the leader but also the desires of the followers."

In order to sustain a mutually beneficial relationship, leaders must know what their people need and want, and then provide it. Give them the (appropriate, effective, correct) tools they need to do their job. Teach them how to use them. Listen to them. It's a simple yet powerful formula.

The Container Store, one of the 100 best companies to work for in 2007 according to *Fortune* magazine, pays its employees 50% to 100% more than the national average. But that's not all. They do more. CEO, Kip Tindell, believes that hiring great people is the first step in ensuring that customer service transcends expectations. He receives more than 30,000 job applications annually; only 6% are hired. Next he provides training—every full-time salesperson receives about 185 hours of formal training in his or her first year, as opposed to the industry standard of about seven hours. The incredible value in training is evident at The Container Store—right down to the bottom line. Revenue for 2005, was $441 million for its 38 locations.

> *"In organizations, real power and energy is generated through relationships. The pattern of relationships and the capacities to form them are more important than tasks, functions, roles and positions."*
>
> **—Margaret Wheatley,**
> author of *Leadership and the New Science*

4. Own-a-Vision. Own-a-Strategy

Great leaders "see" the future. Klaus Kleinfeld, COO of Alcoa, visualizes before he acts. He closes his eyes and concentrates on what he wants to achieve and how he sees it unfolding. He asks himself, "What should this look like?" Only when he has a clear vision in his mind's eye does he start executing his plan.

> *"The leader has to be practical and a realist, yet must talk the language of the visionary and the idealist."*
>
> **—Eric Hoffer** (1898-1983), author

Be clear on where your organization is within a local setting as well as within a global context. In today's global marketplace a vision of both these environments is necessary for successful execution. Articulate your vision, your plan, in simple, and specific language so it will be accurately understood by all involved.

SC Johnson, one of the world's leading manufacturers of products for household cleaning, pest control, and personal care bills itself as "A Family Company," that cares about every family. The current chairman and CEO,

Dr. Herbert Fisk Johnson III, is the fifth generation of the Johnson family to lead the company. Headquartered in the United States, SC Johnson operates in more than 70 countries, acting on its vision to do what's right. The company expounds its commitment loud and clear: "...From the products you use, to the air you breathe, to the community you live in, we're working to make this world a cleaner, healthier, better place—today, for the next generation and beyond." It adds value by proactively executing on issues, like producing green products, conserving critical resources, and preventing dangerous disease—issues that are of concern to its customers around the globe.

What issues concern your company and its customers? How are you addressing them?

5. Demonstrate Integrity and Trustworthiness

Be what you say—whether you are part of a huge corporation or you are a one-man show. Action speaks louder than words.

Imperial Oil, an affiliate of ExxonMobil, feels a strong commitment to business integrity is key to earning and maintaining public, shareholder, and employee trust. It starts with Imperial's commitment to meeting high corporate-governance standards and continues with Imperial's statement of *Standards of Business Conduct* which is used throughout the company to clearly define how business should be conducted.

Employees are encouraged to raise any concerns they might have by using the confidential hotline and mailbox.

Ethics and integrity extends to the reporting of financial and business results. Imperial takes a transparent approach to financial management and reporting. The goal is for financial and operating results to be clearly understood by all involved, so resulting execution will be on target.

Business integrity and trustworthiness knows no size. My roof leaked. Allright Roofing came and fixed it. It started leaking again several months later. The owner, Martin Kuypers, returned to investigate. When he found that he had not repaired the cause of the leak, he returned all the money I had paid him. He said he doesn't get paid because he hadn't fixed the problem. He raised the trustworthiness quotient of Allright Roofing in my eyes about 1000%.

6. Move Ideas to Implementation

Great ideas are just that—ideas… until they are executed. Entrepreneurs may be afraid to implement for a variety of reasons—from believing the "if it 'ain't broke…" philosophy to actualizing their fear of failure. Jim Estill, CEO of Synnex Canada, a wholesale computer distributor, explains,

> It is not the ideas that will make a business successful, it is the implementation. When my company went public, I was worried people would see our statements and public disclosures and copy what we were doing. Some tried. Over time I came to realize that implementation is hundreds of little things that tend to be almost impossible to copy… I have seen more failures caused by inaction than caused by having ideas stolen.

Ideas are moved toward implementation more easily when the organization sees a worthwhile reason for doing so. Companies such as Intel, Google, eBay, and IBM have used their desire to discover something new to move their ideas. Apple and Toyota seem to be driven by the pursuit of ever-better products—and organizations such as Microsoft are ambitious to win and succeed above all others. Determine your purpose to move your ideas forward—it will serve as your impetus to execute.

7. Become a VP of Revolution

Sometimes radical performance improvement is required. Sometimes strong measures are needed to increase morale and motivate people to follow.

"Not everything that is faced can be changed. But nothing can be changed until it is faced."

—James Baldwin (1924-1987), writer

Sometimes cutting-edge ideas are needed to deal with a rapidly changing environment in order to foment change. That is the time for the leader (or someone he's appointed) to become a change-agent, a VP of Revolution.

The skills (both technical and soft) of a good VP of Revolution are many. They must be able to bring together all stakeholders and ensure their support and commitment. They must be able to question company patterns of thinking and working, assumptions about the organization and its environment as well. They must also be able to evaluate the situation from different points of view (those of customer, competitor, employee, partner). They must be able to build a coalition with outside partners. Finally the VP of Revolution must give the people charged with executing the changes a sense of ownership, so they are motivated to continue executing.

"The quality of a leader is reflected in the standards they set for themselves."

—Ray Kroc (1902-1984), founder of McDonald's Corporation

Many leaders of large organizations have of late taken on the mantle of VP of Revolution. Mark Hurd, arriving at Hewlett-Packard on the heels of Carly Fiorina, had vast changes to make. He took a back-to-basics approach, made difficult decisions, stepped away from the limelight, and encouraged a team approach. He managed to renew energy. His bold statement, "execution trumps strategy" says it all.

Randall D. Ponder, in his book, *Leadership Made Easy*, indicates that the specific leadership style of a leader doesn't matter. What is significant is the way leaders work and conduct themselves. If you set high standards, your people will follow you.

Leaders know they must lead—they must implement—they must execute. Leaders know that they must motivate their people to follow them—in order to move ideas to execution. The alternative is just not tenable.

"The three traits of a leader are example! Example! Example!"

—Sam Geist

—— ✳ ✳ ✳ ——

RATE YOURSELF

☐ On a scale of 1 to 10: How well does my organization execute its strategy?

What can improve my organization's execution by one point?

_____

_____

_____

_____

THE BOTTOM LINE

By bringing vision, passion, skills, confidence, and empathy to their changing organization, today's leaders move strategic thinking to strategic doing.

Chapter Four: THE FACE OF THE PEOPLE

What I now know _____

Your people are your frontline. Your frontline is your action line. Your action line is your upper hand. They make it happen. They execute for you.

Your people make it happen for you every day. They are the "actors" in your production. They execute your strategy—your ideas—your plans. How successfully they perform depends a great deal on how well you know them and their capabilities. How satisfied they are depends a great deal on the culture of your organization.

KNOW YOUR PEOPLE

Together with the fundamental shift in the American business model there has been an evolution in today's workforce. According to data from a 2003 workforce study conducted by Harris Interactive and commissioned by Spherion, more and more workers are moving toward a new mindset, (Spherion has dubbed these workers—Emergent), leaving the traditional worker, to fade away. At the time of the study, 31% of the workers interviewed fell into the Emergent category (projected to become 53% by 2007), 21% were considered traditional (projected to shrink to 8% by 2007), and 48% were classified as migrating—that is migrating from a traditional to an emergent mindset (projected to be reduced to 40% by 2007). Do you know your workers? Do you know into which classification they fall? Do you know if they're migrating? Do you really know who works for you?

THE EMERGENT WORKER

Analysis of the study provides a clear picture of this group of workers whose attitudes and expectations differ from their traditional co-workers. They feel more in control of their careers and want job rewards based on performance. They are more concerned with opportunities for learning and growth. For them, loyalty is defined by the value of their contribution to the organization rather than the length of the time they've worked for a company. According to the study they cross all boundaries including age, demographics, education, industry, the size of company in which they work, as well as their position in the organization.

"Candidates relate to the same issues we see identified in the study. They want to know who they would work for, not just the company, but the person, what the culture is like, whether they'll be exposed to new areas, given an opportunity to learn new skills. And there are lots of firm beliefs these days about work/life balance. There is a sense of independence that was much less prevalent in the past."

—**John Wahby**, Senior Vice President, Spherion

Emergent workers feel that where they go to work, who they work for and how they spend their time, matters. Seventy-three per cent of respondents indicated they would be willing to move their careers to the back seat for their families.

THE TRADITIONAL WORKER

Job security, stability and clear direction are of greater concern to the traditional worker than they are to the Emergent worker. Their definition of loyalty is someone who stays for the long haul. As one respondent said, "I like to be sure I'm doing things the right way... the company way."

While 72% of traditional workers felt that changing jobs could damage their long-term career advancement in 2003, 86% agreed to this statement in an earlier study. The trend, even with traditional workers, is that they are less likely to place value on the organization over supervisor or peers, and less likely to place responsibility for their careers on their employers' shoulders.

This survey provides new insights for today's employers, indicating the need for organizations to change in order to become and remain an employer-of-choice. According to the study Emergent workers are happiest in an organizational environment that plays to their strengths and aspirations. If they are frustrated by the limitations a traditional organization imposes, they are unlikely to do well and unlikely to stay. However the study also indicates that a shift to an emergent management style can have a dramatic and positive impact on job satisfaction, trust, loyalty, and performance.

Michael L. Eskew, chairman and CEO, UPS Inc., remembers when he was delivering packages. That experience molded his decision-making, reminding him to ask himself "How would a driver do this?" Consider your people's perspective in mak-

> *"36% of the average company's operating expenses is comprised of labor costs."*
>
> **—Saratoga Institute,** Pricewaterhouse Coopers's human resources-analysis program

ing the decisions that affect them and in executing the plan that is central to your organization. Get to know your people well—really well.

KNOW YOUR PEOPLE'S STRENGTHS AND WEAKNESSES

Recognize their strengths and utilize them. During my presentations on execution, I often ask program attendees if the following statement is *True or False*: "The people who work for you now, are capable of a lot more than you give them credit for."

Almost everyone (89%) reply—*True*. Why is it then, that they don't take advantage of the capabilities of their people?

A client story. Sitting around the conference-room table, the staff at ALPS in Missoula, Montana, were the first to admit they could do better, after they had finally had the opportunity to air their frustrations and discuss the issues that had thwarted their performance. Once grievances were out in the open, staff members felt a huge weight lifted from their shoulders and they set out to demonstrate their true capabilities.

Your people often know more than you, since they live it day by day. Best Buy's store manager in Manhattan (on 44th Street and 5th Avenue) is proof. He noticed that there was a large Brazilian community living near his store. In order to better serve them, he hired Portuguese-speaking employees, who discovered that cruiseships carrying Brazilian passengers docked in New York City. They contacted the travel company, found that the store was of interest to these tourists—and suddenly they had busloads of tour groups coming in on Sundays. Best Buy head office would never have been aware of such an opportunity.

At the other end of the spectrum, be honest to yourself about your peoples' weaknesses, so you don't put them into untenable situations. Know your people so well that you don't set them up for failure.

Another client story. Bill Sousa ran a technology services company. Anticipating continued growth, he felt it would be a good move to open a new division in Beijing, China. Deciding to promote from within, he sent his brightest manager, Tom K., to be its leader. A year later the division was closed. While Tom had excelled under his tutelage, the project Sousa set before him was beyond his scope, and Tom failed miserably. Sousa lost both an excellent manager at home and an opportunity overseas. It is vital to see your people accurately for who they are and who they are capable of becoming.

Marcus Buckingham, well-known management consultant and author, wrote in *First, Break All the Rules* that, "Great managers know they don't have 10 salespeople working for them. They know they have 10 individuals working for them... A great manager is brilliant at spotting the unique differences that separate each person and then capitalizing on them."

SATISFY YOUR PEOPLE'S NEEDS AND WANTS

a) Freedom from Fear

One of the great human fears—the fear of the future, of the unknown, of change, often rears its head. People feel safe when they're informed. Combat fear and its ugly byproduct resistance by providing open and clear communication.

"People don't resist change. They resist being changed."

—Peter Senge, scientist, Director of the Center for Organizational Learning at MIT Sloan School of Management

b) Feeling Important and Worthy

People want to work for an organization that recognizes their value. They want to be respected for their work and they want their work to be meaningful. They want to be listened to for their ideas.

"Brains, like hearts, go where they are appreciated."

—Robert McNamara, former U.S. Secretary of Defense

Evidence suggests the onset of another talent war. Those leaders who are better prepared for combat by really knowing their people are more likely to be victorious. The ability to get and keep the best people is vital, since those best people are the ones who will help their companies move from strategic thinking to strategic doing. They will move your ideas to execution.

RATE YOURSELF

☐ On a scale of 1 to 10: How accurately does my organization know what the staff members want and need? How well does my organization give what is needed?

What can my organization do to improve its knowing and giving by one point?

_____

_____

_____

_____

THE BOTTOM LINE

Understanding the people who work for you—their needs, their capabilities, their fears, their dreams—enables you to successfully lead them in the charge toward effective execution of your business strategy.

MARKETPLACE LESSONS I'VE LEARNED ALONG THE WAY

What I now know _____

The ever-evolving marketplace is a tough no-nonsense teacher—with real life lessons on execution—whether we are ready to learn—or not.

Today's marketplace is full of rewards for those who execute—and full of thorns for those who fail to do so. My travels, my research and reading, and my clients have provided me with marketplace lessons I think are valuable to everyone in business today. I share them in my weekly *QuickBites* e-newsletter and with participants in my sessions. I would like to share a few of them with you, since I'm always reminded that 90% of what we learn is from outside our immediate sphere of influence.

MARKETPLACE LESSON: Innovate

Once upon a time, a lot of imperfect carrots were harvested—sometimes up to 70% of production. They were thrown away or used as pig feed. California farmer Mike Yurosek, a "think outside the carrot patch" kind of guy, couldn't stand the waste. He cut the discarded carrots into two-inch pieces, and then put them into a potato peeler to peel and shape them.

Voila! A new industry was born: baby carrots! Yurosek's innovative action has changed our eating habits. Today we eat more than 10 1/2 pounds of carrots per person a year—almost twice as much as in pre-baby carrot days. They're in kids' lunchboxes, they're on every crudité platter—and they're good for you.

Lesson Learned:

"The opportunity for innovation is everywhere. Find it and move with it. Executing great ideas offers many rewards." —S.G.

MARKETPLACE LESSON: Execute! Execute! Execute!

The Gap in their heyday in the mid-to-late 1990s was where it was at. They were hip. They were trendy. They were the tenant every landlord wanted. No longer.

During the last several years there has been a steady decline. All the experts put their own spin on the reasons for the decline: too much competition—overlapping competitors—fashion-sense miscues. Everyone is a maven, spouting strategies for renewal, but for the time being the situation looks bleak.

In today's fast-moving, global marketplace, no one, no matter how big or how small can pat themselves on the back, figure their business concept is invincible, put their feet up, and relax. The vultures are just too close behind.

Lesson Learned:

"Rule #1 in the marketplace game is that you can never stop. There is no endgame. Keep moving, innovating, changing, executing, re-inventing yourself." —S.G.

MARKETPLACE LESSON: Get Ready to Change

Meeting with a variety of organizations in my travels, I have been hearing more and more frequently that they are creating new positions that reflect the organization's specific goals.

A bank for which I was consulting recently created a "VP of Shared Services" position, with the responsibility to ensure that their internal resources are shared by all departments.

A huge fast-food chain incorporated a "VP of Individuality" position to focus on making this global corporation "feel small."

An airline has developed the post of "VP for the Customer Experience" to improve its interaction with customers at all points.

...And when I did some work for a retail client they gave me the title, "VP of Revolution"—a title meant to encourage change within the organization.

Each in their own way enunciated quite openly what was important both to them and to their customers. What can each of us do to demonstrate our interest in our goals to our organizations, our employees, our customers?

Lesson Learned:

"By creating positions that clearly speak to our culture and our business intent, we can actually move toward becoming who we say we want to be."
—S.G.

PART II:
THE EXECUTION TEAM

Chapter Five: ALL ABOARD

What I now know _____

If your people don't execute—they are not part of the solution, they are part of the problem.

Your people want to be part of the solution—otherwise they wouldn't be working for you. They want to execute your ideas—your plans—your strategy. They want to demonstrate what they can do—but they need to feel comfortable. They need to feel they can trust you. They need to understand the role they are to play.

Execution requires innovative thinking, energy, and trust. Since executing is moving—from old to new, from the status quo to the unknown it's easy to resist the effort. Your employees need assistance to overcome some of the resistance they feel. Discuss it with them. Get it out in the open. This way you can address it and begin to deal with it.

RESISTANCE MAY BE CAUSED BY SEVERAL FACTORS:

- Not understanding the situation well. Not knowing the reasons for the changes, what the alternatives are and what would likely happen if these changes were not made.

- Fear of loss—this includes loss of responsibility, loss of internal structure, loss of position—loss of the work life they have known.

- Not trusting management. Years of hidden agendas, half-truths, exclusion, takes their toll.

"Trust is enormously powerful in a corporation. People won't do their best unless they believe they'll be treated fairly. The only way I know how to create that kind of trust is by laying out your values and then walking the talk. You've got to do what you say you'll do, consistently, over time."

—Jack Welch,
former Chairman and CEO, General Electric

Providing an honest, straightforward explanation may both clarify your plan and provide some understanding that will alleviate their fears. Lack of trust, however, is a more serious problem and requires a more determined approach.

IT'S A MATTER OF TRUST

Recent studies have found that a great number of employees don't believe or trust their leaders. In a 2007 survey, conducted by Discovery Surveys, only 53% of employees said they believed the information they got from senior management. If your people don't trust you, they may be afraid to talk to you—if that's the case, their ideas won't get to the top, and existing problems will continue to fester and grow. (Keep Samuel Goldwyn's comment in mind, "I don't want any yes-men around me. I want everyone around me to tell me the truth, even if it costs them their jobs.") Opportunities are lost. If you don't take the action you said you would take, you are dismissed as not being trustworthy or dependable. What can be done to narrow the credibility gap? What can be done to create an "open" work environment, where employees feel like important partners?

While consulting for staff and management at organizations that maintain an "open" structure, and to experts in the field, I hear the following suggestions reiterated again and again.

• Be Approachable

Be available to listen to ideas, criticism, or differing opinions with an open mind. Be aware of your body language (avoid frowning, shaking your head, folding your arms). It speaks volumes.

• Get Staff Input

Meet informally. Listen. Ask questions. Collect feedback. Be attentive. Use information received wherever possible, and let staff know their contribution is valuable (even if it is not possible to implement their suggestion).

• Hold "Open" Meetings

Consider the points of view, goals, and concerns of all stakeholders. Enable honest, open dialogue, identify problems (for both management and staff) and work together to address and solve the issues. Close the credibility gap. Communicate clearly.

Give employees the opportunity to tell it from their perspective. Provide an environment that enables your people to speak about their thoughts on the quality of leadership, their complaints and frustrations, the obstacles they face. Offer solutions to their grievances or let them know why it can't be done.

• Treat Staff as Partners

Let your people know that they have an important role to play in moving the organization forward. It's a real morale booster and it promotes trust.

"People excel and learn, not because they are told to, but because they want to."

—**Peter Senge**, scientist, Director of the Center for Organizational Learning at MIT Sloan School of Management

It's only by establishing a workplace environment that promotes inclusion rather than exclusion that "knowledge-transfer" throughout the organization happens and effective execution becomes possible. When information is shared among staff, among departments, among branches, silos are eliminated and everyone is enabled to perform better. Employees are much more willing to share with their co-workers in a culture that supports learning, co-operation, and openness.

> *"We need to constantly bring ideas to one another. We don't have any other choice. The world doesn't make exceptions for small companies."*
>
> **—Jack Kahl,** founder, Manco Inc.

Manco, now owned by the Henkel Group, has a huge share of the duct tape market in the United States. Strategists say its unique culture is largely responsible for its success. Goals are posted throughout the company, daily sales are listed on large charts as are shipments, billings, sales and marketing expenses, and monthly profit and loss statements. Signs above the shipping dock shout out: "If you're not proud of it, don't ship it." At meetings it is commonplace for employees to thank people who helped them make a successful presentation to a customer. The company's bi-monthly newsletter, *Duck Tales* even offers tips to managers, including this one: "Hold meetings whenever rumors start... and give employees nothing but honest answers." The Manco organization has grown from a small company to part of one of the largest global companies by giving its people the supportive culture to execute its strategy.

• Listen to Staff

CIGNA Property & Casualty was having a tough time. Its numbers were miserable and management decided they needed to learn more about the problems—from their people. The staff was invited to a brown paper fair.

> *"We were trying to create a climate in which people were willing to step up and announce, in effect, that they were in trouble—which is incredibly hard. But gradually people grew to trust Isom (Gerald Isom, CIGNA P & C, President) enough to know that we didn't want to punish anyone. They saw for themselves that the sooner we knew what was wrong, the faster we could fix it."*
>
> **—Tom Valerio,** former Senior VP of Corporate Re-engineering, CIGNA P & C

In a large multi-purpose room, brown butcher paper was taped all over the walls. On the paper was a flow chart of CIGNA's work process. Everyone in the building was asked to put up anonymous Post-It notes informing senior management what parts of the process worked, what parts didn't, and why.

Some of what came out was new—some wasn't. But almost all of it was bad.

Management was able to see where problems lay—and only then could they begin to correct them. (It took CIGNA five years.) Without engaging in open dialogue with their people, CIGNA could not have begun to execute effectively.

Getting it out in the open—getting everyone aboard has many advantages. It puts everyone on the same page, ready to work together toward executing the same goals.

RATE YOURSELF

☐ On a scale of 1 to 10: How good is my organization at encouraging its people to gladly get aboard the journey to execution?

In what way can my organization involve its people in order to improve its rating by one point?

_____

_____

_____

_____

THE BOTTOM LINE

Recent research indicates that out of every dollar of an organization's expenses, on average about 40 cents is spent on staff. Not connecting honestly with staff, not utilizing their capabilities efficiently, is economic suicide, since it doesn't enable execution to take place.

Chapter Six: ENGAGE THEM

What I now know _____

Highly engaged employees outperform—out-execute less-engaged employees right down to the bottom line.

There's a glut of business literature concerning employee engagement (or disengagement)—and with good reason. Research has found clear links between the level of employee engagement and their innovation, motivation, and their focus on customers and the organization's financial and operational goals. We need highly engaged employees precisely because their performance enables our success. Effective execution begins with engaged people!

> *"Engaged people are proud to work for the company. They are committed to stay and put in extra effort to facilitate the company's goals."*
>
> **—Soni Basdi,** Senior Project Director, Chicago-based HR and consulting firm, ISR

While there are differences from study to study, research shows that highly engaged employees outperform their disengaged counterparts by 20 –28%. With statistics such as these (and those that follow), it is easy to see why it is essential for leaders to determine the level of engagement that exists in their organization and implement strategies to facilitate full engagement.

> *"Start with the assumption that quality makes money, it doesn't cost money. And start with the assumption that the worker knows more about the job than anyone else—or he or she shouldn't be doing it."*
>
> **—Peter F. Drucker** (1909-2005), writer, management consultant and university professor

A recent 12-month study by HR research and consulting firm ISR, of more than 664,000 employees from 72 companies analyzed three traditional financial performance measures. Included were net income growth, operating income, and earnings per share growth (EPS).

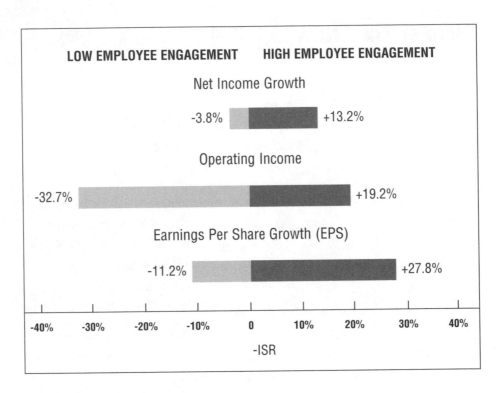

MOTIVATE ENGAGEMENT

Most employees are enthusiastic when they begin a new job. They come on board ready to do their best. They want to succeed. However an attitude survey of more than one million employees conducted by Sirota Survey Intelligence finds that in about 85% of the companies interviewed, employees' morale drops sharply after their first six months—and continues to deteriorate for years afterwards.

> *"A person who's truly engaged says… 'I'm willing to give a little bit more. I'm willing to help my team member when I see they're in need [or] I'm willing to clean without being told by my manager.'"*
>
> —**Tim Galbraith,** Vice President of People Development, Yum Brands Inc.

Motivate engagement by understanding each person's unique abilities, skills, motivators and work styles. Adopt a managing style that focuses on the "person," not just on their position.

PRAISE AND RECOGNITION MOTIVATE ENGAGEMENT

Praise, recognition and positive reinforcement are powerful motivational tools. Give them liberally and freely. In a recent interview, Dr. Guy Beaudin of HRH International Company, a psychological consulting firm to corporations, emphasized the value of praise. "As a leader, part of your role is to increase the behavior that will enable you to execute a new strategy, serve customers better, improve results. And clearly, behaviors that are positively reinforced tend to be repeated."

"Starting today, thank at least five people a day. A handshake, a personal note, or a greeting card will do wonders to boost morale. People who feel appreciated become energized. They work harder, wanting to exceed their goals and prove that they can do even better."

—Duck Tales, Manco Inc. newsletter

Give on an ongoing basis. It shouldn't be just a once-a-year-at-review-time activity. There's no downside to this. It works for all companies—not only for leaders of large companies.

GIVE PRAISE

Deliver praise as soon after a praiseworthy action has taken place, verbally or in writing—mentioning the specific action. Deliver praise with sincerity and enthusiasm, avoiding repetition of the same tiresome phrases (like "nice job") again and again. Give praise on its own. Don't include a qualifier or a negative add-on (like "but, if only.")

GIVE RECOGNITION

Recognition is a powerful form of affirmation. It gives your employees the reason to continue—to push a little harder—to do a little more. Asking employees for their input in important issues elevates their self-esteem. Solicit input face-to-face or by email or surveys, then listen to ideas and take them seriously.

Give the gift of your own time. Respect your employees' time. Rather than just dropping in, make an appointment to see them—and they'll view their time as valuable as well. Take them out for lunch.

When former CEO of Southwest Airlines, Herb Kelleher talks about what he has learned along the way, he mentions that people should be respected for who they are, not for the title or position they hold. As a sign of respect he listens to what all people have to say.

"You don't have to have a doctorate to have an idea... show that you care about them [your employees] as individuals, not just as workers... if I'm talking to a person, that person is the only person in the world while we're talking."

Recognize achievement publicly—at a meeting, in a newsletter, informally to other employees for even more impact.

GIVE AUTONOMY

Make employees feel trusted enough to be given a degree of independence.

WestJet, an airline based in Western Canada, gives frontline staff the authority to decide whether to issue travel credits to customers who have gone through problematic travel situations. Goodwill is generated for customers—and with employees.

GIVE REWARDS

Rewards, even small ones, make a big splash. A day off, the right to leave early or arrive late, are appreciated rewards for work well done. Sunflower Market, an organic and natural food retailer, has a break-room with a sign on the door that says "napping encouraged." Steinmart, an upscale, off-price specialty store chain has a choice parking spot in front of each of its stores for the monthly top employee. WestJet executives send handwritten notes for excellent performance and include a movie pass or a $10 gift certificate.

GIVE FEEDBACK

If you want improvement you must give feedback—honest, positive, relevant, detailed feedback—as close in time to the performance as possible. Use the formal annual employee appraisal only to summarize the year, not to surprise the employee.

"The task of a leader is to get his people from where they are to where they have not been."

—Henry Kissinger,
former U.S. Secretary of State

TECHNIQUES TO IMPROVE YOUR FEEDBACK

- Give specific, unemotional, and focused comments about the performance rather than the employee.

- Give positive feedback publicly. Applaud.

- Give appropriate criticism for poor performance privately with suggestions for improvement, but also give positive feedback for performance that warrants it.

- Give feedback that encourages improvement, focusing on the do-able. Outline strengths and skills.

- Follow-up verbal feedback with an email or a note. Make certain feedback was correctly understood and will be acted upon.

- Use an effective adult-to-adult feedback style, not a parent-to-child mode that creates employee defensiveness and alienation.

GIVE TRAINING

Often companies don't train for fear that employees will leave and take their new skills with them. Consider what happens, however, if you don't train them and they stay. Skills training, cross-training, and continuing education—even if they're not entirely job-related—demonstrate to employees that you are interested in their personal development. Improving performance by offering one-on-one coaching, providing mentoring, or reorganizing the job around employees' special strengths is certainly rewarding for the employee. Men's Wearhouse has replaced most of their traditional training methods with an apprenticeship model, which has been found to be much more effective. Store managers are encouraged to demonstrate effective sales techniques and to coach employees to develop personal selling styles of their own—styles that they feel comfortable using.

GIVE GROWTH OPPORTUNITIES

The lack of future opportunity is the number one frustration of younger top performers. While 85% of employees say career growth is a key reward for them, a Towers Perrin study finds that only 49% of respondents say their organizations provide it.

Those companies that take a personally-interested-in-their-employees approach—from the hard currency (fair pay), the soft currency (praise, respect) and the right currency (training, mentoring) perspectives—will have the best and brightest executing their plan. Re-evaluate your reward-and-opportunity-giving strategies to determine if the best and the brightest are to be found in your company.

DISENGAGEMENT HURTS

A recent Gallup poll noted that actively disengaged workers cost U.S. organizations between $292 billion and $355 billion a year. That's frightening. Disengagement claims almost one-fifth of the workforce.

Even more frightening are the statistics from international consulting company, Kabachnick Group, indicating that poor performance by co-workers is the number one reason that dedicated, caring and engaged

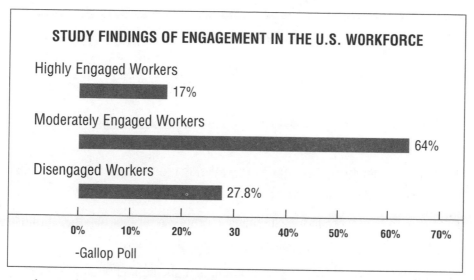

employees leave their jobs. That's a double-whammy for any organization. Not only are the cream-of-the-crop gone—but those who remain are disengaged and executing poorly.

Disengagement is not an all-of-a-sudden phenomenon, nor is it caused by only one factor. Most often disengagement grows over time and is the result of several factors:

- Employees find they have little or no control over their work environment, and no involvement in decisions, or in the changes in the environment.

- Employees have no opportunity to advance, learn, or contribute. They lack future opportunities.

- Employees receive no recognition for their contribution. Eventually they lack pride in the job they've done.

- Employees receive ineffective communication.

Research indicates that disengagement is much easier to prevent than it is to remedy once it is ingrained.

EIGHT TIPS TO DEFUSE DISENGAGEMENT

1. Stay connected. Coach employees continually about how to improve their performance. Teach new skills, strategies, concepts.

2. Communicate clearly, directly—using both appropriate verbal and body language.

3. Focus on employees' strengths. Pay attention to the "quiet" people. (They know more than they say). Give them an opportunity to be heard.

4. Position employees in the situations appropriate for them by measuring their skills, preferences, beliefs, values and personality.

5. Watch for behavior changes during the first six months of employment. Performance improves or deteriorates during this period.

6. Provide informal feedback on a regular and frequent basis, offering suggestions and asking employees for their job-related feelings and ideas.

7. Invite top performers to meetings they would not normally have the opportunity to attend.

8. Recognize your own strengths and weaknesses as a leader, utilizing those strengths that will engage employees and minimizing those weaknesses that will create disengagement.

Companies are adopting more informative employee-engagement surveys in place of simple job satisfaction assessments in an effort to better determine what is turning employees off and they are using the information to create programs to bolster that engagement. Getting and keeping engaged employees starts with providing an inclusive culture at the top of the organization. It develops and grows when employees are viewed as valuable assets rather than as costs.

When Howard Schultz founded Starbucks, he was more interested in creating the right work environment than he was in the price of coffee. He wanted to attract and retain people with values like his own. As he commented in *Fortune* magazine, what tied Schultz to his people "was the dream of building a company that would achieve the fragile balance of profitability, shareholder value, a sense of benevolence, and a social conscience." He has certainly succeeded.

Organizations have often thought that having deep pockets was the answer to their people-management issues. However today's work environment has clearly demonstrated that both soft and hard currency are needed to drive employee engagement—and the company's success at executing forward.

"Unfortunately, they [employees] often find conditions that block high-performance, such as excessive bureaucracy, burying them in paperwork and slowing down decision-making to a crawl. Or, they work in an atmosphere where management is consumed with finger-pointing, rather than co-operative problem-solving... removing obstacles to performance would enormously improve the competitiveness of U.S. companies. Performance can be improved by between 20% and 40% at most companies if these obstacles were removed."

—**Dr. David Sirota,** Chairman Emeritus, Sirota Survey Intelligence

RATE YOURSELF

☐ On a scale of 1 to 10: How well does my organization engage and satisfy its employees?

What new satisfiers can my organization provide to bring its rating up one point?

_____

_____

_____

_____

THE BOTTOM LINE

Your people want to perform—to achieve. They want to be engaged. Your responsibility is to create the environment that enables them to do what they wanted to do all along—so you can get what you wanted all along—execution in your organization at every level—from top to bottom.

Chapter Seven: TEAM THEM UP

What I now know _____

Teamwork is more than two words stuck together...
much more. Teamwork enables you to execute your strategy.

Teamwork is the driver that pushes strategy and ideas to implementation. Even though it is tough to develop a hardworking effective team, our heavily team reliant workplace (a recent survey of Fortune 1000 companies reported that the firms of 83% of respondents use teams) behooves us to build a better one—a high-performance team that gets us to where we want to go.

THE TEAM LEADER

Every team needs a leader. When you're the one in charge, your success depends on understanding and accepting your role as a leader, understanding and accepting the various personalities, capabilities and skills within the team and leading them to successfully execute. No matter your title, whether it be team leader, manager, or facilitator,

TEAMWORK

A man was lost while traveling through the country.

As he tried to reach the map, he accidentally drove off the road into a ditch. Though he wasn't injured, his car was stuck deep in the mud.

So the man walked to a nearby farm to ask for help.

"Warwick can get you out of that ditch," said the farmer, pointing to an old mule standing in a field. The man looked at the decrepit old mule and looked at the farmer who just stood there repeating, "Yep, old Warwick can do the job." The man figured he had nothing to lose, so the two men and the mule made their way back to the ditch.

The farmer hitched the mule to the car. With a snap of the reins he shouted, "Pull, Fred! Pull, Jack! Pull, Ted! Pull, Warwick!" And the mule pulled the car right out of the ditch.

The man was amazed. He thanked the farmer, patted the mule, and asked, "Why did you call out all those other names before you called Warwick?" The old farmer grinned and said, "Old Warwick is just about blind. As long as he believes he's part of a team, he doesn't mind pulling."

—Adapted from James W. Moor—*Some Folks Feel the Rain: Others Just Get Wet*

you are responsible for helping your team achieve the goals set before them. Yours is a juggling act!

As leader, your role is to set the stage and clarify the vision, concentrating on the "what-to-do" and the "why-do-it" and adopting a long-term view.

As manager your role is more task-oriented, concentrating on the "how-to-do-it," and adopting a short-term day-to-day view.

As facilitator, your role centers around involving all group members, concentrating on helping the team function in the present, and assisting them to articulate their views. How do you know which role to use at any given time? Lead your group, manage the daily work and facilitate decisions—and you'll be doing your job.

EIGHT PRINCIPLES TO BUILD A GREAT TEAM

Principle #1: "Determining our common destination, determines our common destiny together."

See a united vision. Visualize as a team, deciding what the goals are to be, so there is a buy-in from all members.

Principle #2: "All of us together can do more than each of us can do alone."

Develop common goals. Members will be committed to common goals when they recognize and are recognized for their contribution. Develop common goals. Members will be committed to common goals when they recognize and are recognized for their contribution.

Principle #3: "Each of us has our own role that fits into the whole undertaking."

Clarify roles and responsibilities. Make certain that each member fully understands his or her function in the group. In any business situation clarity about one's role and responsibilities is of paramount importance. In a group it is exponentially so.

Principle #4: "Let's go… let's go… let's really go."

Be a cheerleader: give support. No team is an island. The leader must be the conduit for ensuring that resources, assistance, information, and applause flow to the team, through the team, and out again.

> *"Change job descriptions to job responsibilities."*
>
> —Sam Geist

Principle #5: "Competing divides us; co-operating multiplies us."

Live co-operation! Work co-operation! The skills and abilities of each team member must be complementary to those of others and be used for the good of the project. Success belongs to the team. Think baseball.

Principle #6: "Listen twice as much as you talk."

Facilitate open and honest communication among members. Give team members timely information. Encourage diverse opinions and ideas. Listen.

Principle #7: "Teamness matters."

Value team members. It improves performance, improves self-worth, improves work life, improves project outcome.

Principle #8: "Mediate: reconcile each team member's perspective."

Resolve conflict. (Conflict arises from differences—in power, values, attitudes and goals.) Address differences directly to minimize their negative impact. However, keep in mind that conflict in work teams is not necessarily destructive. Conflict can lead to new ideas and approaches and can offer a renewed interest in dealing with problems that have arisen.

> *"By design and by talent we were a team of specialists, and like a team of specialists in any field, our performance depended on both individual excellence and on how well we worked together. None of us had to strain to understand that we had to complement each others' specialties; it was simply a fact, and we all tried to figure out ways to make our combination more effective."*
>
> —*Bill Russell,* legendary basketball star

> *"There's no limit to what can be accomplished when nobody cares about who gets the credit."*
>
> **—John Wooden,**
> retired American basketball coach

A high-performance team taps into hidden potential, enabling future stars to shine. It enables "quiet people" to grow into their capabilities and share their skills. It improves productivity, solves problems, and enables execution. The benefits of a great team justifies the effort to create it.

Top Five Characteristics of a Good Team

- The entire team participates actively and positively in meetings and on projects.
- The team listens to and offers thoughtful feedback to speakers.
- The team trusts the judgment of members. Dissenting opinions are heard and considered.
- The team is willing to take risks.
- Team goals are realistic and have realistic time frames.

Top Five Characteristics of a Good Team Member

- Shares feelings, ideas, opinions openly and honestly.
- Is open to new ideas and suggestions from others, listens to speaker's point of view.
- Encourages development of other team members.
- Respects and accepts individual differences, resolves conflict openly.
- Understands team goals and is committed to them.

> *"Talent wins games, but teamwork and intelligence wins championships."*
>
> **—Michael Jordan,**
> retired professional basketball player

MasterCard wanted to find an advertising campaign to narrow its gap with Visa, so McCann Erickson (its prospective new advertising agency) created a team of three creative-types who "were very comfortable working together, so we debated everything freely." After intensive brainstorming they came up with the "Priceless" award-winning campaign—which is still "priceless" today.

General Foods felt it had to respond faster to market changes and opportunities so it set up a nine-person team with a mandate to develop a new product. It hoped this would take less than the five to seven years it usually takes to move from concept to shipping. This high-performance team had Jell-O Pudding Snacks desserts in grocery stores nationwide within three years, which was fast enough to establish marketplace dominance.

Teamwork may not be a panacea for all that ails an organization, but when strategically built and deployed, a team has the power to make "1+1=3" a reality. It has the power to execute.

"Men work together, whether they work together or apart."

—Robert Frost
(1874-1963), American poet

———— ✳ ✳ ✳ ————

RATE YOURSELF

On a scale of 1 to 10: How well do teams work in my organization?

What changes need to be made within the organization to improve the teamwork rating by one point?

_____

_____

_____

THE BOTTOM LINE

When both the task(s) to be accomplished and the processes of the group work are recognized and addressed, teamwork empowers today's businesses to execute.

MARKETPLACE LESSONS I'VE LEARNED ALONG THE WAY

What I now know _____

*The ever-evolving marketplace is a tough no-nonsense teacher—
with real life lessons on execution—whether we are ready to
learn—or not.*

MARKETPLACE LESSON: Find the Right People

My son-in-law was recently wooed to a new job—and with it came the
responsibility of revamping his department. He was to let the old guard go.
Hire new blood.

He's a young guy, and he wanted to get his department into shape as
quickly as possible. However, he is also a smart guy—he wanted to make
the most effective long-term changes—to hire well.

He realized he needed to do more than just replace the old people and
get new people. By getting the right people in the right place he would be
able to successfully execute his vision and his strategy. He made the
changes slowly and thoughtfully.

Lesson Learned:

"Your most important asset as a leader is not just 'any people'—it's the
'right people.'"—S.G.

MARKETPLACE LESSON: Make A Connection

I finally rented the 2005 film, "Memoirs of a Geisha," based on Arthur Golden's acclaimed novel. There were two CDs in the case—the first was the film, the second was interviews with Golden and director Rob Marshall along with other behind-the-scene glimpses. What struck me most from these interviews was the enormous effort Golden made to research the life of a geisha extensively in order to pen his novel accurately and honestly. And then again there was the huge effort Marshall made to ensure that the geisha world he created resonated with the viewer.

I thought of how much work, time and consideration went into creating a vision that is real for the viewer—that pulls the viewer in and connects with him or her. Then I wondered how much research we undertake, how much effort we make to really discover who our associates, partners, employees, and customers are so we can forge meaningful connections—and strong bonds with them.

Lesson Learned:

"Whether in Hollywood or at the workplace, a connection based on interest, similar goals and accurate information is vital to forming an authentic relationship that enables execution of the plan."—S.G.

MARKETPLACE LESSON: Give The Tools To Do The Job

My wife decided to help me out by cutting the grass on the weekend. She added gas to the mower's tank, pulled the cord, and started the mower. She was doing a good job and was quite proud of herself when, half way through the job the lawn mower sighed and stopped. Nothing we did could convince it to start and eventually we gave up.

Thinking about Rene's disappointment at being unable to complete her job, I realized that in business just as in life, people are enthusiastic about their jobs—and they want to do them well.

Lesson Learned:

"It is up to us to give our employees the most effective, "in good order" tools so they can do what both they and you want—to get the job done."—S.G.

PART III:
EXECUTION SKILLS

Chapter Eight: COMMUNICATE CLEARLY

What I now know _____

Monologuing is out! Dialoguing is in! Clear effective communication is a powerful link between ideas, strategies, and plans and executing them successfully.

CLEAR COMMUNICATION

When CIO Insight asked 792 information-technology senior executives in an on-line survey what skills define a strong leader, 65% of those who responded cited effective communication skills as their first choice.

Whether the communication comes from the corner office (or anywhere else in the organization) it correlates directly to greater employee satisfaction and increased productivity. Every endeavor that requires action or change should include a clear communication plan that explains both the idea and its goals to employees in a meaningful way.

A recent report by Watson Wyatt Worldwide found that effective communicators keep employees informed about the needs and reasons for organizational change; share business plans and goals; and reward performance that supports those goals.

This result in higher employee engagement levels, lower turnover and stronger financial returns for the organization.

"Employees have a right to fair and accurate communication... because they have a personal stake."

—Rajesh Subramaniam,
President, FedEx Canada

Results of the 2004 study, "How to Get Your Employees to Walk the Talk," conducted by Discovery Surveys, and involving more than 50,000 employees at 60 organizations, found that about 40% of employees didn't

"Simplify! Simplify! Simplify! Don't use 12 words when you can use six words; don't use six words when you can use three words."

—Sam Geist

understand their organization's goals. Many of those surveyed didn't understand how their work contributed to the organization's objectives. According to Bruce Katcher, industrial and organizational psychologist and author of the study, "they don't see the big picture. They don't recognize that no matter what their role in the organization is, they can be contributing to its goals, vision and brand." If they don't see the big picture—if they don't recognize their contribution, how can they possibly execute the plan effectively?

As a leader it is your responsibility to speak (and write) in language that is clear and concise and to ensure your people do as well. Plain language is not about dumbing down information—it is about expressing yourself in accessible terms. Referring to several annual surveys, Robert Half, chairman of Robert Half International Inc. says, that esoteric language and jargon like "paradigm," "metrics," "value-added," "get on the same page," and "core competency" are annoying and overused. "People have to understand your meaning. Listeners benefit when a speaker takes the time to explain why a particular deal is successful rather than summarizing its success as a 'win-win' situation." What are you doing to ensure that spoken and written communication circulated throughout your organization is accurate and that its effectiveness is measured?

The Mission of Southwest Airlines

Southwest Airlines is dedicated to the highest quality of customer service delivered with a sense of warmth, friendliness, individual pride and company spirit.

To Our Employees

We are committed to provide our employees a stable work environment with equal opportunity for learning and personal growth. Creativity and innovation are encouraged for improving the effectiveness of Southwest Airlines. Above all, employees will be provided the same concern, respect and caring attitude within the organization that they are expected to share externally with every Southwest customer.

If a company is unable to define clearly and crisply the value it provides internally to its own people, it is difficult to imagine that the value it provides is clear to its customers. Southwest Airlines communicates its mission statement in less than 100 words.

Its values sound out loud and clear. Employees understand them. They believe in them. They share them. They are able to act on them.

Use the form of communication to keep in touch with employees that works best for you and your organization— whether it be the company newsletter, the intranet, regular employee meetings, the phone or face-to-face discussions. To become a better communicator ask someone you trust to critique both your written and verbal communication. Ask employees for their feedback as well. You will then have an idea of what everyone's thinking.

"The art of communication is the language of leadership."

—**James Humes,** author

AS CLEAR AS MUD

One of the greatest communication problems is assuming that your message is clear and has been accurately understood. Follow-up often finds the opposite to be true. John Britnell of Britnell and Associates, a financial-services client of mine, was frustrated. However diligently he communicated, he felt the initiatives he was trying to introduce were going nowhere. He asked if I would visit his offices, talk to some of his team leaders, and assess the situation. I checked with Michael R., the head of one department, and he explained to me what he perceived his responsibilities were. He felt his team was doing a good job of executing the plan presented to them.

"The greatest problem with communication is the assumption that it has taken place."

—**George Bernard Shaw** (1856-1950), playwright, social commentator

When I checked with William B. the source of the instructions, I discovered he had intended Michael R. and his team do something entirely different. While Michael R.'s team may have been doing a great job—it was not the job they were supposed to be doing.

Everybody, Somebody, Anybody, Nobody

*There was an important job to be done and **Everybody** was asked to do it.*

***Everybody** was sure **Somebody** would do it.*

***Anybody** could have done it but **Nobody** did it.*

***Somebody** got angry about that because it was **Everybody's** job.*

***Everybody** thought **Anybody** could do it, but **Nobody** realized that **Everybody** wouldn't do it.*

*It ended up that **Everybody** blamed **Somebody** when actually **Nobody** asked **Anybody**.*

—Anonymous

"After all, when you come right down to it, how many people speak the same language even when they speak the same language."

—**Russell Hoban**, writer

I also found this situation to be evident in other companies with which I consult. When brick walls are gradually erected between corporate and regional offices or between the VP of Marketing and the VP of Operations (who may, indeed, have offices next door to each other), miscommunication develops and grows. Miscommunication has been shown to consume up to 45% of organizational energy—and according to James Clarke, business coach, consultant and trainer, two out of every three mistakes occur because of miscommunication.

COMMUNICATE EFFECTIVELY

It takes more than assertive speaking. It takes more than trust, honesty and openness to make a real connection. It takes active listening—using eye contact, body posture, facial expressions and tone.

It takes practice to communicate proficiently. "Communication often determines whether a project succeeds or fails," says Kirsten Hale of Global Knowledge in *Training* magazine. "Project managers need to know the most effective way to communicate both up and down the organizational chain to a variety of audiences, and how to manage and influence people who don't directly report to them." Accurate communication really does enable accurate execution.

Of the many suggestions I've tried, I find these to be most helpful.

1. Mimic your listener in your communication style to demonstrate empathy. (Speak slowly when they speak slowly, be animated when they are animated).

2. Use "I" statements, such as "I feel (disclose your feelings) when (state the behavior non-judgmentally) because (clarify the result on you)." (Example: "I feel stressed when the work isn't done, because I know John will be upset with me for not making sure it was completed.")

3. As a listener, use reflective listening by restating the feelings and information that have been communicated to you. Use appropriate non-verbal cues.

4. As a listener ask a few well-chosen open-ended questions to facilitate receiving more information.

> *"A good listener is a good talker with a sore throat."*
>
> **—Katharine Whitehorn,**
> journalist, author and columnist

> *"He who speaks, sows. He who listens, reaps."*
>
> **—Argentinean proverb**

J.B. Hunt Transport Services, realizing the importance of communication skills, has provided communications training for project managers. "Coming from technical backgrounds they know what needs to be done and are skilled at doing it, but they aren't always aware of the necessary level of communication with stakeholders or team members required to run a project effectively," says Phil Kindy of J.B. Hunt.

The most effective communicators keep employees informed—even if the news is bad. Nobody likes to deliver bad news, but it should be treated the same way good news is treated—with accuracy, honesty and transparency. A study of communication ethics released in 2005, by the International Association of Business Communicators (IABC) found that employees would much rather hear the straight goods—good or bad—

than be kept in the dark or be fed a "spin-doctored" version of the events.

Rajesh Subramaniam, president of FedEx Canada, a recipient of the IABC's award for excellence in communication leadership, takes communication seriously. He connects with employees when it is convenient *for them*—even at two or three in the morning, if employees are working the overnight shift. He ensures systems are in place so front-line employees are informed and engaged. Communication is a key component of his business decision-making—and hence his execution.

Several years ago, the physical landscape of office space began to change. Many executives found that the old model—private offices mixed with cubicles, wasn't conducive to teamwork. It's not conducive to good communication either. Today, with teamwork often the modus operandi, the open-concept office space also enhances communication. Don Crichton, VP of Workplace Solutions at HOK Canada, comments that "companies realized they'd be more productive if employees were interacting with one another rather than working in isolation."

No matter what we do, when we interact with other people, we are communicating. Clear communication is a valuable business (and personal) advantage, as it affects relationships, performance and the speed and accuracy with which ideas and plans move into execution. How well

> *"The most important thing in communication is to hear what isn't being said."*
>
> —**Peter F. Drucker** (1909-2005), writer, management consultant and university professor

we communicate is a direct correlation to how well we execute.

RATE YOURSELF

☐   On a scale of 1 to 10: How good is my organization's communication to employees? To customers?

What can be done to improve its communication to employees by one rating point? To customers by one rating point?

_____

_____

_____

_____

THE BOTTOM LINE

Communicating effectively is more than just transmitting or receiving information accurately. It is about making powerful and beneficial connections that enable execution to take place.

Chapter Nine: FOCUS-FORWARD...
NOT ON THE PAST

What I now know _____

If we were supposed to be constantly looking backward we would have been created with eyes in the back of our heads. Execution requires a forward focus.

Our natural inclination is to use our past experiences as a barometer for our thoughts and actions. Looking backward stalls us out. It limits our ability to think future-focused and act future-focused. It's difficult, if not impossible, to move forward, while living in the past.

"The only thing that keeps you from succeeding in the future is your ability to unlearn what made you successful in the past and the speed with which you can do that."

—Lucia Quinn, Executive Vice President, Boston Scientific Corporation

Vivek Paul, president & CEO of Wipro Technologies, said the best advice he ever got was from an elephant trainer near Bangalore. Trekking through the jungle, Paul saw some large elephants tethered to a small stake. He asked the trainer how he was able to keep such large elephants tied up this way. The trainer replied, "When the elephants were small, they tried to pull out the stake and they failed. When they grew large they accepted the stake as a part of life and never tried to pull it out." For Paul it was a clear reminder that old expectations anchor us to the past.

LOOK FORWARD. ACT FORWARD

Executing our strategies aggressively requires that our actions are focused on the future. When the past comfortingly beckons, try this little mind trick to move yourself to the present—where you live, work, and play.

"Looking backward will get you run over today."

—Malcolm Baldridge
(1922-1987), U.S. Secretary of Commerce

Focus on what you can do right now, forcing your mind to let go of the past in order to concentrate in the here-and-now. Should your thoughts wander back, do some self-talk. Remind yourself "That's in the past. Now I'm focusing on my goals, executing the strategy to which I've committed myself." Never let yesterday use up too much of today. Concentrate on the things that move you toward your goal.

GE has set for itself the goal of solving some of its customers' toughest environmental problems. "Ecomagination," the plan to reach this goal puts into practice GE's belief that financial and environmental performance can work together to drive company growth, while at the same time solve some of the world's biggest challenges. Looking toward a greener (and profitable) future globally, GE is committed to excelling in four areas—practicing clean research and development, increasing revenue from Ecomagination products, reducing greenhouse-gas emissions, and communicating openly with all stakeholders. GE has let go of yesterday to invest its efforts and resources in an economically and ecologically sound future.

"You can never plan the future by the past."

—Edmund Burke (1729-1797), 1791 (in a letter to a member of the National Assembly)

For years Dell had been a very successful manufacturer of affordable, quality PCs. However, past achievement is not enough. Competition from HP, Compaq, Lenovo, and Gateway encroached on its territory. Marketshare declined. Dell had to revitalize its strategy to regain some of its lost customers.

In the spring of 2007 Dell began making profound changes and taking well-thought-out risks to move the company to the next level—making information technology affordable to millions of customers around the globe.

In a memo to all its employees it outlined the new platform "One Dell, One Focus—Simplifying IT for Our Customers."

Dell outlined some of the steps it was going to execute to make its goal a reality:

- Fix our Core Business to be competitive.

- Re-ignite growth in our Core Business to reach more customers.

- Build for the long-term to provide more customer solutions.

- Embark on a bold, long-term initiative to radically simplify IT for customers.

Dell recognized its shortcomings and was prepared to focus forward. It involved its people by launching "Idea Storm," which invited employees to offer up ideas and suggestions. At the same time it also involved the entire community. It invited Dell customers (and potential customers) to jump into the eye of the storm by "telling us where you would like to see us improve, push the boundaries and try something new." Instead of trying to hang onto the past, Dell was grabbing hold of the future by executing to reach its goals. What is your organization doing to grab hold of the future?

> *"I try to learn from the past, but I plan for the future by focusing exclusively on the present. That's where the fun is."*
>
> **—Donald Trump,**
> entrepreneur and author

BREAK DOWN BIG GOALS

Breaking down your major goals into smaller short-range objectives enables both you and your people to see the face of success more frequently. Ongoing achievements build confidence, reinforce a positive attitude, keep momentum going, and ensure goals will be met.

Keep a spotlight on your quarterly, monthly, or even weekly performance goals with visible reminders—a large white-board calendar, a weekly email, a Friday-

> *"It is not enough to take steps which may someday lead to a goal; each step must be itself a goal and a step likewise."*
>
> **—Johann Goethe** (1749-1832), author

morning "rah... rah... rah" meeting—whatever works for you. Measure these smaller goals against your long-term objective, to ensure you maintain your future-focus and continue to move forward. Regular and frequent communication with the people who are working to achieve the goals you set before them, is beyond vital as previously mentioned.

RETELLING "REFRESHES"

While you are focusing on your future goals, it may be warranted and valuable to occasionally retell your vision, your plan to your people.

> *"By keeping goals visible and focusing on them, we force ourselves to make innovation happen."*
>
> **Tom Corbo,** former CEO, Manco Inc.

On their fifth anniversary, *Fast Company*, a magazine "committed to telling its readers what's new, what's next and what matters... and inspiring them to think bigger and instruct them on how to do better," decided to restate its purpose. "We will continue traveling into the future with you, making sense of this epic journey, charting the changes as they come. And we'll continue to do so without compromising the core principles that define the mission of FC—and without altering our commitment to you." Such a powerful statement of purpose revitalizes, refocuses and renews *Fast Company* and its connection with its readers. Retelling your statement of commitment to your employees—and to your customers strengthens your connection with these two valuable partners. It encourages and stimulates a forward focus rather than a backward gaze. It encourages and stimulates execution.

RATE YOURSELF

☐ On a scale of 1 to 10: How much does my organization focus on current goals, rather than on yesterday's triumphs or regrets?

What strategies can my organization use to move its focus forward by one rating point?

_____

_____

_____

_____

THE BOTTOM LINE

Use your future-focused vision, your innovative outside-the-box thinking, your smarts to direct your execution strategy forward toward your goals.

Chapter Ten: HIRE AMBASSADORS

What I now know _____

Ambassadors execute—assassins don't.
Which your employees are depends to a great extent upon you.

Ambassadors help build your relationship with customers. They help build your business and your bottom line. They execute your strategy. Assassins destroy your relationship with customers. They destroy your business and your bottom line. They drive customers away—and you pay them to do it!

"You're either part of the solution or part of the problem."

—Eldridge Cleaver, author and American civil rights leader

GOOD HIRING MAKES FOR GOOD BUSINESS

Good hiring practices ensure that new hires feel their capabilities and personalities are compatible with the company, with their work and with their co-workers.

They feel they're a "good fit." They become loyal. They stay. They're in sync with your goals. Unfortunately this scenario is often not the case. A survey of 860 employees from 32 retail companies conducted by retail productivity specialists, Terri Kabachnick & Company Inc., found:

- employee turnover is the single largest hidden cost in retailing

- 76% of senior management said low productivity by middle management and the frontline is their biggest challenge

- 72% of management who hire have never acquired interviewing and profiling skills

- only 22% of companies measure turnover

- 83% of managers hire people they like rather than matching people to jobs

- less than 1/3 of the retailers surveyed use hiring tools such as interactive computer testing, job profiles, behavior and belief assessments, and selling/service profile assessments (of the companies using such tools, 96% reported significant decreases in turnover).

> *"I've been blessed to find people who are smarter than I am, and they help me to execute the vision I have."*
>
> **—Russell Simmons**, entrepreneur, co-founder, Def Jam Recordings

No matter the industry, high employee turnover is the result of not getting the right people and not getting them into the right jobs. This situation obstructs productivity and execution.

While getting the right people and getting them in the right jobs may be challenging, it's absolutely necessary. When Howard Schultz, chairman of Starbucks talks about advice he received, he mentions that to become a great leader it's vital to recognize the skills and traits that you require but don't possess to build a world-class organization and then hire with that in mind. Joe Liemandt, CEO of Trilogy, concurs.

> *"In 10 years, we will see many companies fail because they haven't planned ahead and are unable to find the people they need to run their businesses."*
>
> **—Jeffrey Joerres**, CEO & Chairman, Manpower

According to Liemandt, "One of the most important lessons we learned is that hiring for raw talent isn't enough. We had to build leaders." Liemandt's comments remind me of the legendary quote of advertising guru, David Ogilvy: "If each of us hires people smaller than we are, we shall become a company of dwarfs. But if each of us hires people who are bigger than we are, we shall become a company of giants."

HIRE THE BEST CANDIDATES

Managers in companies with low turnover look for individuals whose beliefs, values and behaviors match those of their company and the job.

The closer that match, the better the fit. Dell is a good example. Michael Dell says, "While we bring in people with strong relevant expertise, we never forget that they must also fit into our culture." Not an easy task.

Five suggestions from the experts to ease the way:

1. Put candidates in front of the job (instead of talk, talk, talk, in front of the interviewer). Introduce them to your team and let them show you how they would do it. Even if they may not yet be skilled at the new job, a good candidate asks the right questions.

2. Hire for abilities, not for specific knowledge of systems or tools. A good candidate can learn specifics with a little help.

3. Give your manager and team members first contact with candidates. Let them be the candidates' first impression of your company, since that's where they'll be working. You aren't hiring people to work on an island. Their work, their attitudes, their behavior, affects everyone around them. Engage in a little "interviewing by wandering around." Encourage team members to conduct informal, casual mini-interviews and report back to you.

4. Take into account how well candidates prepare for the interview. With today's access to information on the Internet, candidates with initiative should be able to arm themselves with considerable information about your organization—and should be able to discuss company issues thoughtfully. (Unprepared candidates show a lack of interest in your company and the job.)

5. "Google" your prospective hire. The Internet keeps no secret. Make reference checks the responsibility of the hiring manager. A reference call from one manager to another is very different from an HR call. Ask "If you could have Joe work on your team again, would you hire him?" While the answer is important, it is the hesitation or enthusiasm with which the response is made that is so telling.

RETENTION MATTERS...

...Right down to the bottom line. How well you handle new employees during their first three months on the job determines whether they become productive, long-term staff members or part of the turnover dilemma.

PREPARE TO RETAIN

- greet new employees in the lobby on their first day

- assign new employees to a clean, well-prepared work area

- detail expectations for the first week and outline objectives for the next three months

- allow for a period of growth, keeping expectations reasonable

- ask new employees to identify skills they need/would like to develop to assist them in their jobs

- arrange for skills training, peer coaching or job shadowing

- schedule monthly performance-feedback sessions.

"Surround yourself with the very best people, and spend a lot of time trying to create a common sense of purpose—a mission—and an environment in which people can have an opportunity to realize their full potential."

—**Stanley O'Neal**, CEO, Merrill Lynch

The costs linked to the loss of talented employees are staggering—estimated at 50% to 150% of the departing employee's annual salary. What does turnover cost you? There's also the loss of the future potential of the employee, loss of customers loyal to departing employees, and loss of confidential information about operating methods, technology and clients to competitors who have hired the employee. Of even more concern is the resulting "loss" of execution of the organization's goals and strategies.

A recent survey conducted by the Bureau of National Affairs found the median turnover rate at 16% annualized, to be the highest in two decades. How does your turnover rate compare? As it continues to escalate it behooves companies to find a solution to this draining problem, especially as it is more common among the most valuable top performers of an organization.

Traditionally, organizations use data from exit interviews to determine why employees are leaving, and they use that information to develop initiatives to promote retention. Unfortunately this method can only offer up strategies that might retain other employees.

In order to be more proactive, companies have begun to utilize employee surveys on an ongoing basis in order to collect frequent feedback as well as to develop effective retention strategies. Surveys provide employees with an anonymous opportunity to share information about their jobs, managers and organization. This enables the company to identify the key issues that push employees to consider leaving. With this information in hand, management can implement strategies to retain employees.

ISR's (International Survey Research) Key Driver Analysis, conducted across 22 companies in various industries, prioritized employee responses to questions about their intention to leave. The top three reasons given for leaving, in order of importance, are:

1. lack of individual development

2. lack of career advancement

3. lack of recognition and rewards

Use these findings as an excellent starting point to address the vital task of retaining your ambassadors.

REDUCE TURNOVER

In the fast-food industry, turnover rates of 200% are not unusual. Some companies like Starbucks are tackling the problem with higher hourly wages. It says its turnover rate is between 80% and 90%. David A. Brandon, CEO of Domino's Pizza doesn't agree with this retention tactic. He feels "you can't overcome a bad culture by paying people a few bucks more." He commissioned research that showed the most important factor in store success was the quality of the store manager. When there was high turnover in this position, the ripple effect was enormous.

Look within your organization to see where your high turnover is located and why—and implement the methods to stem it.

> *"As employees, we're not possessions of companies. We're all free agents. If it's easy to steal [an employee] from company ABC, then company ABC isn't doing a good job making it a great place to stay."*
>
> —**Michael Palmer,** Executive Director, HR Services, Ceridian Canada

Domino's began focusing on its store managers and attacked turnover in this position. It hired more selectively (starting by conducting an online evaluation of prospective managers' financial skills and management style), coached managers on how to create better workplaces (by working and learning with staff, and by keeping track of their best and worst performers), and motivated them with the promise of stock options and promotions (by giving options based on criteria such as sales growth and customer service and profit-linked bonuses). And it seems to be working. Turnover has dropped by about 35%. Not only that, leadership at Domino's has become stronger, its business plan shows growth and it is able to execute its long-term goals. Keeping in mind that employees are your most valuable resource, hiring well and retaining good people are vital moves toward achieving *your* long-term goals—and executing your long-term strategies as well.

SAS Institute has developed a powerful employee-focused culture based on a simple idea: satisfied employees create satisfied customers. With low employee turnover—consistently and significantly below the industry average—SAS reaps the rewards of employee loyalty and benefits from the work of the most talented minds in the software business. In return, employees work a 35-hour week, have two subsidized on-site childcare centers, an employee health-care center, wellness programs including on-site massages in a high-stress workplace, a huge fitness and recreation center, subsidized restaurants… and so on. SAS has created an environment that executes its strategy by ensuring that employees feel like valued members of a community. While the costs may be high, SAS says it saves $67 million a year in avoided turnover costs.

Hiring well plays a vital role in your business success. It must be undertaken with the knowledge that the results of your hiring decisions absolutely affect the future of your organization—and its ability to execute productively and profitably.

RATE YOURSELF

☐   On a scale of 1 to 10: How effective are the hiring practices of my organization?

What can be done to improve these hiring practices by one rating point?

_____

_____

_____

_____

THE BOTTOM LINE

Human capital offers the ultimate driver for success. Attracting and retaining the best and the brightest enables you to execute gloriously.

Chapter Eleven: DELEGATE—DON'T ABDICATE

What I now know _____

When you delegate skillfully, you challenge and stimulate your people to execute.

Leaders direct, plan, organize, analyze and innovate—but they don't do the jobs they've hired someone else to do.

DELEGATE EFFECTIVELY

Delegating effectively increases productivity. Leaders agree with this—yet many are reluctant to let go. Your time is limited. Spend it on the work that only you can do. Find the most valuable contribution you can make to your company and focus on that role. Do that well. Own that job. Delegate everything else.

> _"Never tell people how to do things. Tell them what to do and they will surprise you with their ingenuity."_
>
> —**General George S. Patton** (1885-1945), U.S. army general

Delegation is a company-grower. It's a confidence-builder. It's the way to develop and mature employees. It's the way to get your strategies and ideas executed. How are you ever going to know your employees' potential if you don't give them a chance to show you?

There may be times when employees are reluctant to accept the job you've delegated to them. They are afraid, they're busy—they may feel they don't have the skills. Perhaps they aren't receiving enough feedback to help them judge how well they're doing.

Avoid reluctance by delegating to their strengths. Don't set them up to fail. Give them the time to effectively undertake the project. Give them the tools so they're able to execute. Give them support. Give them frequent

> *"Get the barriers out of the way to let people do the things they do well."*
>
> —**Robert Noyce,** founder, Intel

feedback so they know how they're doing. (Use the suggestions for giving effective feedback in Chapter 6, page 45).

STAY THE COURSE—DON'T DISAPPEAR

When questioned about strategic execution, Dr. Laurence Hrebiniak, an author and professor at the Wharton School of the University of Pennsylvania criticized leaders and high level managers, saying that once they have done the so-called smart work, (developing the strategies, the ideas, etc.) they turn to their subordinates and say, "Here, execute this... . It's important that the CEO, just like all managers, have a hand in execution." Stay connected. Stay informed. Remain a vital member of the team, giving support, redirecting resources, helping to correct a deterioration in quality, or finding out why productivity has taken a downturn. A leader needs to be present to applaud victories as well as to be on the lookout for problems.

> *"ACCOUNTABILITY: Who does what by when."*
>
> —**Sam Geist**

Businessman and author, Larry Bossidy, writing in the *Harvard Business Review*, commented that while good managers delegate, there are three circumstances that should prompt them to get involved: when somebody is falling behind in their commitments; when important personnel matters arise, particularly if there is a conflict; and in a crisis. He pointedly reminds his people, "Just because you're an executive vice president doesn't mean you don't have to work anymore."

Do your thing—and then step back and resume your leadership position. Give your people the clear message that you trust them to do their work effectively. Let them know that you have passed ownership of the project over to them. Let them know they are accountable for its success. It is under these circumstances that your people can execute confidently.

MICROMANAGEMENT IS POISONOUS

The opposite of abdication is microman-agement. This ineffective management style of emotionally (and sometimes physi-cally) squashing your employees is counter-productive. It's belittling, frustrating, and destructive to the employee, your relationship with the employee, and your company.

> *"We don't want to rub the edge off everybody to the point that the whole place is round."*
>
> —**Jack Welch,** former Chairman & CEO, General Electric

A building management client of mine, built up his business because he was a hands-on person. He took care of all the details in the day-to-day running and long-term planning of his business. He was successful, and his company grew. When it became too large for him to manage it him-self, he hired talented employees, but he continued to stay intimately hands-on—so much so in fact that he didn't allow his new staff to do their jobs. He was unable to change his management style to reflect his new business situation. His employees felt over-managed and under-trusted. Eventually they (and others he hired to replace them) left. He found no alternative but to downsize his business so he could once again manage it alone.

When you think of yourself as part of the team, with each member having very specific responsibilities, you will recognize that delegation is one of your most important responsibilities.

TEN TIPS FOR SUCCESSFUL DELEGATION

1. Ensure you are well versed in the project before you delegate it.

2. Give the job to someone who is capable of getting it done. (The first step in the project may be training or educating your employee).

3. Make sure your employee clearly understands the purpose of the work and knows what the expected outcomes and results are. Encourage questions and provide precise answers.

4. Work out a plan. Include the resources required, all the information needed, the goals to be attained.

5. Set a realistic deadline that is agreed upon by everyone involved in the project. Create a buffer period to allow for the inevitable hiccups and revisions.

6. Be available. Field questions. Monitor the process. If you feel the job is not moving along as you expected, provide assistance. Give instruction. If you feel the job is being done well—stand back, don't hover.

7. Be prepared to provide additional resources and/or assistance mid-project. If needed, reorganize the project into smaller sections so there will be successes to celebrate along the way.

8. Don't tell your employees how to do the project. Give them the opportunity to use their creativity.

9. Keep track of the delegated work, especially if it is a small project that is part of a larger one.

10. Show lots of appreciation (praise and credit) when the project has been completed.

BE A COACH

"My weakness is that I haven't done enough day-to-day coaching and mentoring."

—**Meg Whitman**, CEO, eBay

Successful delegation and effective coaching go hand in hand. Everyone needs a coach—a frank friend or colleague to support their growth and development—someone who will help them to develop greater self-awareness, to improve their skills, to take on new responsibilities and to execute effectively.

Too many bosses are selfish about developing their charges. My son-in-law, Jacob, tells this valuable story. When he started out at Quaker Oats, Jacob had a manager who performed well but realized he wasn't going to move higher in the echelons of management. He took Jacob aside and told him he felt Jacob could go far, and he would do whatever he could to help him reach his potential. He remained very interested in Jacob's development and assisted whenever he could. He was the mentor who enabled my son-in-law to be the success he is today.

A recent study in Great Britain revealed that 80% of managers believe that in order to do their jobs better, they would benefit from coaching or more coaching in their workplace.

The areas in which they felt they would be particularly interested in coaching opportunities were cited by participants:

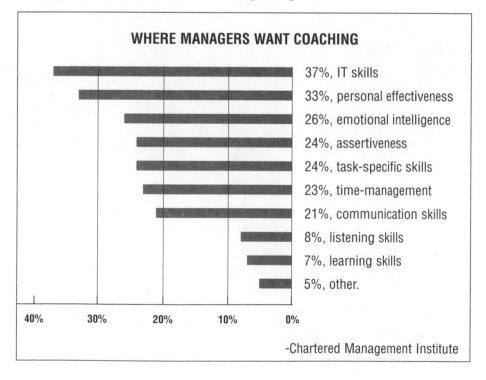

WHERE MANAGERS WANT COACHING

- 37%, IT skills
- 33%, personal effectiveness
- 26%, emotional intelligence
- 24%, assertiveness
- 24%, task-specific skills
- 23%, time-management
- 21%, communication skills
- 8%, listening skills
- 7%, learning skills
- 5%, other.

40%   30%   20%   10%   0%

-Chartered Management Institute

In the same study, although it was found that 14% of organizations do conduct executive coaching and 5% of organizations do have a coaching program solely available to senior management, an overwhelming 93% of managers believe that coaching should be made available to all employees.

Coaching is integral to your delegating process. It creates a comfort zone that is most conducive to executing with assurance. Successful coaching relies on a range of skills, not just supplying specific information and techniques. It especially requires great communication skills such as: questioning, listening, and giving constructive feedback.

Delegating provides an excellent vehicle to move your execution plan forward, because it gathers momentum from all those who take your plan and push it to the next level.

RATE YOURSELF

On a scale of 1 to 10: How well does the delegation process work in my organization?

What can be done to improve the delegation process in my organization by one rating point?

_____

_____

THE BOTTOM LINE

At the end of the day, delegation serves four functions: it gives you the time to make your own valuable contribution; it gives your people an opportunity to grow and develop; it allows you to be recognized as being good at getting results through others; and it provides an effective vehicle for execution.

Chapter Twelve: MAKE MEETINGS WORK

What I now know _____

Meetings work as valuable "execution-organizers" if they are well planned and sharply focused.

"MEET" TO EXECUTE

To germinate new ideas, to overcome challenges, to share information, to organize the execution process, companies spend an inordinate time in meetings. As long as meetings accomplish their objectives of moving ideas to implementation—to execution, they are valuable. However, according to a recent survey of 2,800 executives and meeting attendees, more than two-thirds of respondents replied that 25% to 50% of the time they spend in meetings is wasted.

Since meetings seem to be a necessity today, make them work. Meetings must be fast, focused, participatory, and decisive. Eliminate the "boring factor." Make them crackle with energy, enthusiasm, and passion.

Design a meeting that meets both task-oriented needs (presenting information, fostering collaboration, developing plans, and strategies) and social needs (the need to belong, achieve, communicate, and build a common vision).

> *"The first meeting was held in the Garden of Eve. Eve called the meeting to order but hadn't distributed an agenda. Adam wasn't prepared to discuss the apple issue. The snake kept interrupting the meeting, playing devil's advocate. Jumping to the easiest alternative, a hastily sprung plan was put into action. Today, we live with the ramifications of that first ineffective meeting."*
>
> **—George Huyler,** Executive Vice President, Chief Personnel Officer, IRMC

Organize the *meeting content* to address the task-oriented needs and the *meeting process* to address the social needs.

THE MEETING CONTENT FOCUSES ON TASK-ORIENTED NEEDS

1. Be clear about the meeting's objective:

    - articulate the objective statement clearly at the onset

    - ask if the objective has been met at the end of the meeting.

2. Create a solid agenda:

    - prioritize agenda items in order of importance to the largest number of participants

    - assign a realistic time budget to each item. Stay on track, avoid distractions.

3. Be prepared:

    - advanced preparation by all involved allows the meeting to move smoothly, eliminates wasted time, and facilitates progress to the next step.

4. Follow-up the meeting:

    - develop a culture of accountability, making it unacceptable to show up at the next meeting with an incomplete actions-to-take list. If participants still seem unable to follow through independently, the meeting leader needs to follow up with participants between meetings to ensure action items are being moved ahead.

"Processes don't work, people do."

—John Seeley Brown,
researcher in organizational studies

THE MEETING PROCESS FOCUSES ON THE PEOPLE

1. Choose participants appropriately.

    - Ask yourself: Whose input is needed? Whose input is needed to make a decision? Whose buy-in is needed to move forward? Use your answers to determine which participants are appropriate and necessary.

2. Take the most important expecta-
    tions of the process and turn them
    into agreed-upon factors.

    "Extra long is for suits, not meetings."

    —**Jane Dale**, author, *The Obvious*

    - Some helpful agreements include:
      • having agenda distributed—and read—beforehand

      • determining length of meeting

      • starting and ending meetings on time

      • honoring differing points of view

      • allowing no interruptions

      • speaking openly, honestly and confidentially.

3. Clarify the decision-making procedure to ensure that partici-
    pants' decision-making behavior is consistent with their
    expectations.

    - The three basic decision-making procedures are:
      • autocratic (leader decides)

      • democratic (majority rules)

      • consensus (all agree to move forward before deciding).

4. Decide who will run the meeting. Decide the leader's role.

    - A participative format allows the leader to state the meeting's
      objective and have another team member facilitate the discussion
      (this format encourages everyone to participate).

5. Determine role assignments at the start of the meeting to engage
    everyone in the process and validate expectations and contributions.

    - Important roles include:
      • facilitator (mediator)

- recorder

- leader

- participants

- timekeeper (if a concern).

Meetings are the "what" of an implementation plan. It is here that all the aspects, all the pieces of the plan are discussed and organized. Also needed are the "who" as in who is involved, "when" as in the timing, "how" as in the approach(es) to take, and the final "what" as in the outcome—all of these components are decided at meetings.

"WHO" EXECUTES THE PLAN

The "who" is everyone—from the leader to the employees who execute the details. In order for employees to perform well, they need to be involved, updated, feel they are part of the progress, as mentioned earlier. John Chambers, CEO of Cisco, for example, spends a great deal of time listening to his employees. He attends a variety of events from monthly birthday breakfasts, where employees can challenge him on industry or company issues, to Q & A sessions in every city where he travels. He ensures his employees feel involved and part of the Cisco team, so they will execute the plan effectively. Execution can't take place if any of the "who" are left out of the loop.

"WHEN" IS IT TO BE EXECUTED

The "when" is the time frame for implementation. Establishing a clear-cut time frame assists you to follow the tasks and duties you delegate to all participants sequentially. It also stimulates action and accountability by outlining specific deadlines by which time the work must be completed. Both the commencement of the initial action and the long-term time commitment of the plan should be laid out so execution is timely.

Priorities need to be set in conjunction with the charted timeline, ensuring that highest priorities are accomplished first. This facilitates continued achievement along the line. Employees should be aware of, and agree to, the priority ranking established.

To assist in ever-forward movement, establishing interim goals (milestones) may be worthwhile, especially when the final goal remains a great distance away. List your interim goals with their appropriate (or necessary) deadlines. Ensure interim goals are achieved in priority by highlighting the benefits to be accrued by completing each of them.

Your timetable shouldn't be carved in stone. Always review the schedule you've set to make certain it continues to be applicable.

"HOW" IS IT TO BE EXECUTED

The "how" is the approach (or approaches) taken to achieve the desired results. Various processes may be used, depending on the structure of the organization and the objectives to be reached. Find the process(es) that works best in your situation.

"Because we're so connected to the end product while it's being done, we pick up on all the idiosyncratic things that normally get overlooked by architects. It saves a lot of time and money down the line."

—**Peter Gluck,** architect

Architect Peter Gluck has redesigned the business of building houses by developing and using an integrated process in his architectural firm. Instead of the traditional, architectural design process in which the architect completes design and construction drawings and hands them over to the contractor to execute (often resulting in miscommunication, delays and costly mistakes), his firm now handles a project from beginning to end. The process shift has brought about changes not only in the building stage, but also in the drawing and drafting stage, because now design and construction *really* must work together.

"WHAT" IS THE RESULT

The final "what" is the outcome that is the culmination of the process, where the hand-shaking and back-slapping is conducted—before it is time to move forward again. Perhaps the most important concept to remember as you continue to execute is that the marketplace is dynamic. Change is ongoing. There will always be changes in staff, in products, in techniques, in needs, in technologies. You must constantly be executing in order to revamp and redo as necessary. In fact there should be execution processes in place to handle this inevitability.

RATE YOURSELF

On a scale of 1 to 10: How effectively do meetings in my organization function to push the execution process along?

What can be done to improve the meeting process in my organization by one rating point?

_____

_____

_____

_____

THE BOTTOM LINE

By creating and organizing both effective meetings and effective meeting follow-up you ensure that your ideas are executed.

Chapter Thirteen: DECIDE—DON'T STALL OUT

What I now know _____

Doing nothing is making a choice. Execution can't happen until you decide.

PROCRASTINATION HURTS

Waiting until there are signs of trouble before you move, before you attempt to motivate employees, to execute your strat-

> *"Procrastination is the thief of time."*
> —**Edward Young**
> (1683-1765), 17th century English poet

egy, probably makes it too late to do anything effective. Studies have shown that the best way to hold onto a successful marketplace position is to stay ahead of the curve, continually transforming your organization from a position of strength, rather than playing catch-up. Apple provides an excellent example of an organization that is always expanding its offerings—and re-inventing the ones it has.

Maintaining such a marketplace position requires making smart, swift decisions, day-in and day-out. It requires consistent execution in order to keep the idea-to-action loop closed. Sounds straightforward. So why is it so tough to make decisions—and then follow them through?

Take that first step to getting unstuck and moving forward by understanding why we don't want to decide at all, why we tend to procrastinate. Then take the second step by determining how to conquer

> *"Inaction, contrary to its reputation for being a refuge is neither safe nor comfortable."*
> —**Madeleine Kunin,** 77th Governor of Vermont, Swiss-American diplomat

it. Psychiatrists say that procrastination may be caused by fears—part of the emotional baggage we carry around with us. To overcome your fears—

the fear of failure—the fear of success—the fear of completion, identify it. Name it. Confront it. Imagine the consequences of your actions (or non-actions) as objectively as possible. Although you may still be afraid, if your goal is worth pursuing, you'll be able to act despite the fear.

People also procrastinate for many reasons other than fear:

- They lack commitment to the project or assignment. (*Action-to-take*: look conscientiously for the benefits of doing the work—then begin).

- They don't feel the project or assignment is a top priority. (*Action-to-take*: make a to-do list. Set priorities on the list. Check off as each task is completed so that even hated grunt work gets done and even small tasks are acknowledged).

- They don't know enough about the project or assignment. (*Action-to-take*: gather the information—then begin).

- They have a compulsion to do everything at once. (*Action-to-take*: focus. Stop jumping from one task to the next. Complete one task before moving on).

ARE YOU A CHRONIC PROCRASTINATOR?

In addition to the obvious, "I always put work off until the last minute" and "I'm always late," check off everything that applies to you.

☐ Do you often avoid decisions?

☐ Do you make big plans but fail to carry them out?

☐ Do you avoid trying something new?

☐ Are you staying in your job despite being unhappy because of fear of making a move?

☐ Do you tend to get sick when you have a task you don't want to do?

☐ When you don't get something done, do you blame others for it?

☐ Do you avoid arguments?

If you habitually put things off, and also answered "yes" to two or more of these questions, you too may be a chronic procrastinator.

"You don't drown by falling in the water; you drown by staying there."

—**Edwin Louis Cole** (1922-2002), founder, Christian Men's Network

DECISIONS! DECISIONS! DECISIONS!

Today's business environment dictates that we must decide now and decide fast and decide well. Yet a survey by Teradata, a leader in data warehousing and analytic technologies, finds that more business complexity and more data has made good business decision-making even more difficult. About 70% of respondents said that poor decision-making is a serious problem for business, eventually affecting a company's reputation, long-term growth, employee morale, productivity, and revenue.

"Speed and real-time decision support matter because, when you have the customer on the phone or in front of you, or have a truck in the loading dock, you want to make sure that the right data is available so that the best decisions can be made on the spot."

—**Bob Fair,** Vice President, Chief Marketing Officer, Teradata

It seems to me that despite the severe consequences of procrastinating it is hard to adopt better decision-making strategies because our decision-making process is a habit—and habits are hard to change. Habits make us feel comfortable.

"The chains of habit are too light to be felt, until they are too heavy to be broken."

—**Warren Buffet,** CEO, Berkshire Hathaway

We usually decide on the pleasure or pain (emotional criteria) principle.

However when making important decisions, relying only on emotional gauges can create major stumbling blocks.

At the other end of the spectrum sits the "Rational Decision-Making" strategy. This based-on-reason process includes identifying objectives, gathering facts, analyzing alternatives, and outlining the best course of action. While it has been touted as an excellent strategy for making smart decisions, and it sounds infallible, it hasn't proven to be effective all the time.

How then are we to make the decisions that must be made to begin executing? Getting stuck in lots of data and never deciding (often called "paralysis by analysis") doesn't work, but neither does disregarding valid data and relying only on our intuition. The secret to an effective decision-making process, it seems, lies in maintaining a balance between the rational camp and the intuitive-thought camp.

Based on consultations I have undertaken to assist clients improve their decision-making process I have found that the following steps provide a useful framework for making effective decisions.

TEN STEPS FOR EFFECTIVE DECISION-MAKING

1. Define, as specifically as possible, what the decision is that needs to be made.

2. Identify the goals to be achieved by your decision.

3. Think intuitively. Get in touch with your "gut reaction."

4. Accumulate information, but not obsessively. (If you wait to collect every piece of data, very often it will be too late to make a decision.)

5. Outline the actions to accomplish your goals.

6. Identify the pros and cons for each of the actions. Monitor each option from both a rational and an intuitive perspective.

7. Enlist the assistance of others. Brainstorm. Multiple voices increase the options and broaden the perspective from which to view the situation.

8. Do a reality check. Decide which alternative suits you best, suits the situation best, suits your organization best.

9. Make an intuitive judgment about the best action to take.

10. Make the decision stick by attaching the means to execute it.

Cadbury Schweppes, among other large corporations, attaches a formal performance contract as the final step of strategic decision-making. It specifies the resources (time, talent and money) required to execute the strategy, as well as the financial results that management promises to deliver.

> *"The future doesn't just happen— it's shaped by decisions."*
>
> —**Brad Anderson**, CEO, Best Buy

MOVE DECISIONS FORWARD

Each decision must "have legs" to become executable. The "how?" must be very specifically answered in a clear, step-by-step approach that is apparent to everyone who comes in contact with the decision.

> *"Specific outcomes require specific actions."*
>
> —**Sam Geist**

An action plan that facilitates decision follow-through, can take any number of physical formats—: a large calendar-type whiteboard listing all the actions to be taken, by whom, using what resources, by when, with what expected results and actual results listed; a computer-generated spreadsheet that is emailed to all involved, revised daily/weekly, and emailed again; regular meeting discussions and follow-up reports; a flow-chart; even a row of sticky notes. Use the format that works best, but use some instrument that enables visible, do-able follow-through. And then wait no longer. Take action. Execute.

At one time Xerox senior management had lost touch with its customers. The decision was made to get back in touch and the subsequent action plan that was devised, assigned the 500 major accounts around the globe to top Xerox executives. Each executive, including the chief accountant, the general counsel and the head of human resources, was responsible for executing the decision. They successfully regained contact with those important customers only by taking charge and executing the mandate set before them.

> *"When you get right down to the root meaning of the word 'succeed,' you find that it simply means to follow through."*
>
> —F.W. Nichol,
> Vice President and General Manager, IBM

Whole Foods' core values enable the follow-through of decisions. Each staff member belongs to a team that meets regularly to discuss issues, solve problems, and listen to each other's contributions. In the store, staff interact, smile, are delighted to help customers and stock shelves because everyone feels they are appreciated and part of the Whole Foods team. No job is too menial to execute well.

Assertive decision-making instigates execution. It is the key to transformation. It is one of the significant character traits that differentiates high-performers from poor ones. As I always remind my audiences, "You can fix a bad decision, but you can't fix indecision."

— ❋ ❋ ❋ —

RATE YOURSELF

☐ On a scale of 1 to 10: How effective is the decision-making process of my organization?

What can be done to improve the decision-making process of my organization by one rating point?

_____

_____

_____

_____

THE BOTTOM LINE

As a leader you must get off the fence. Deal with it. Execute. Move your organization forward faster by assuming your responsibility to make good decisions.

Chapter Fourteen: MEASURE WHAT MATTERS

What I now know _____

Measuring what matters enables the right things to get done—enables the plan to be executed.

The purpose of measuring is to drive the business forward—to stimulate continuous improvement and execute the goals of the business.

Sun Microsystems Inc., providers of computers, computer components, software and information-technology services, assembles real-time data on the amount of time its system is available (or unavailable) to its customers (that is system uptime or downtime) at their sites. They use the data to determine the causes of downtime as well as to educate people and improve its processes. Sun Microsystems does whatever it takes to maximize its customers' uptime (which maximizes those customers' ability to serve *their* customers).

Sun Microsystems measures what matters. It measures what is important to its customers—uptime.

> *"You can be sure our plan was perfect; it's just that the assumptions were wrong."*
>
> **—Kenneth Olsen,** former CEO, DEC (Digital Equipment Corporation)

In order for measuring to give you reliable, usable information, it must be concrete (not abstract), accurate (not estimated), and real (not wishful thinking). You cannot manage or improve or change what you cannot measure.

The good news is that many organizations do measure their progress, the bad news is that either much of the measuring that gets done is not of the right things, or the measuring results are not utilized.

MEASURE WHAT MATTERS

Take this four-step approach to ensure that you measure what really matters, not just what your current information system happens to track regularly.

1. Identify the metrics that are critical for your business

Every business has key drivers for success. These drivers must be understood, measurements must be developed to assess them and attention must be focused on them.

SAS Institute, a major producer of software, recognizes that employee recruitment and retention are their key measures of performance. With this in mind, James Goodnight, CEO strives to hire and retain the best people. SAS then creates systems to ensure all employees feel equally valuable and important whether they develop systems or serve food. SAS measures its success against the number of employee applications it receives annually (34,761) and the percentage of voluntary turnover (4%).

> *"GM would have known that it was failing ten years before it did if it had tracked customer defections."*
>
> —Frederick Reichheld, Bain & Co.

Singapore Airlines measures training, where it spends 15% of its payroll costs. (Weigh this against the 2006 State of the Industry Report, in which the American Society for Training and Development estimated that corporations would spend more than 2.5% of payroll on training in the coming years, compared with 2.2% three years ago.) Even more significant is the fact that its commitment to training is so strong that this is also tracked.

Of course there are many other metrics worthy of measuring, such as manager proficiency, leadership capability, percentage of sales from new products, and customer service. Because customer service probably has the greatest impact on your overall business performance it is frequently measured.

My two personal measurement favorites are: customer repeat rate and customer referral rate.

2. Develop and implement internal and external benchmarks

Standards against which you can compare your metrics are valuable. Use them to determine whether your performance is improving or not. Use them to compare yourself to your competitors.

Benchmarking data is available from various sources, from consultants to industry associations. The American Productivity and Quality Council (APQC) has been operating a long-term research project called the Open Standards Benchmarking Collaborative, which enables participants to compare more than 100 processes across a range of industries.

But as with internal measurements, no matter how useful benchmarking can be, it will ultimately prove to be a waste of time and money unless its findings are implemented.

"We stumble across the truth from time to time, but most of us pick ourselves up and hurry off as if nothing ever happened."

—*Winston Churchill* (1874-1965)

KleanUp, a cleaning-products company, found that its sales-per-rep ratio was lower than those of its competitors. Upon investigation, it discovered that staff lacked sufficient understanding of the benefits and features of some of its newest products. An action plan, developed to improve training and staff communication, was successful in increasing sales, as well as growing the confidence of the reps.

3. Set up business processes to address measurement findings

Processes that reach across the entire organization work best. When information and data are shared, it helps to ensure that it gets to the right people at the right time. The mission of Mothercare in the United Kingdom is "to meet the needs and aspirations of parents for their children, worldwide" through the wide variety of maternity wear, nursery furniture, accessories, infant clothing and bedding that it sells. However due to a high percentage of part-time employees and a high labor turnover rate, Mothercare had problems delivering on its goals. The measurements it put in place enabled it to identify and address these problems. As a result, Mothercare focused on hiring more full-time employees. As well, the company implemented both a 10-week introductory training program, and an extensive "expertise training" program to develop proficiency in a particular product line. Two or three times a year there are refresher courses. Everything is measured—even the impact on sales when employees return to the stores after training. By closing the loop between measurment and action, Mothercare has been able to fulfil its mission.

4. Focus on results

The ultimate goal of measuring is to use the results in order to move strategies to execution. It is a tool intended to help companies improve. Measuring what matters is important, but using the findings to improve is vital. At the end of a Princess cruise that my wife and I took, the cruiseliner distributed a lengthy questionnaire concerning the service onboard, which my wife dutifully filled out. Since there were a couple of areas she felt the liner needed to improve, she offered to expound on her answers by telephone—and she included her phone number.

> *"Worry about being better; bigger will take care of itself."*
> —**Gary Cooper,** founder, Land's End

While the liner professed that they wanted to improve (hence the questionnaire), they never called or acknowledged her answers in any way.

In the early 1990s Andy Taylor, now chairman of Enterprise Rent-A-Car, had been hearing more complaints than usual from customers about his company's service. His team of senior managers designed a new customer-service survey that asked for seventeen responses, and included an open-ended "How could we have served you better?" question at the end. The first version of the survey didn't produce the needed results. Too long. It was revamped. In its final format it asked only one question: "Overall, how satisfied were you with your recent car rental from Enterprise?"

It contained five boxes, so customers could check off the appropriate response to this question—from "completely satisfied" to "completely dissatisfied." The company calculated the percentages of check marks in each category, calling the scores the Enterprise Service Quality Index (ESQi). This measurement process was refined... and refined... and refined yet again—scores were measured within local areas and eventually the survey was switched to phone surveys to speed up feedback. Management started taking ESQi seriously. ESQi has become an inextricable part of Enterprise's corporate culture. Whenever a customer indicates any dissatisfaction on the survey, a fix-it process goes into play. Branch managers call the customer, apologize, try to find the root cause of the disappointment, and then develop an appropriate solution. By closing the loop, Enterprise has seen both a drop in customers who reported negative experiences as well as a huge increase in those customers who report positive experiences and provide positive word-of-mouth recommendations. Enterprise continues to operate and grow according to the plan it executes.

> *"When solving problems, dig at the roots instead of just hacking at the leaves."*
> —**Anthony J. D'Angelo**, author

Hunter Douglas, maker of window fashions, includes a warranty card in all its products. It too asks questions of customers, and like Enterprise it has instituted a detailed process, the goals of which are threefold: to fix any problems immediately; to involve the dealer so they're aware of problems; to follow-up with the customer so they will feel comfortable enough to purchase Hunter Douglas products again and to recommend the company and its products to their friends. Hunter Douglas has also enjoyed great success by measuring customer satisfaction and by taking appropriate action to ensure customers are indeed satisfied.

Every company has the opportunity to create a measurement system for services or products—and thereby take advantage of ways to positively connect with its customers.

Larry Bossidy in *Chief Executive* summed up "measure what matters" well. "To grasp real opportunities in the marketplace you have to set targets and timeframes and then measure how you are complying with the targets. You don't get successful execution unless you're meeting those targets."

RATE YOURSELF

☐   On a scale of 1 to 10: How well does my organization measure what matters?

What can be done to improve my organization's measuring by one rating point?

_____

_____

_____

_____

THE BOTTOM LINE

Problems can't be solved until you know what they are. Measuring helps to identify the problems—and offers you an opportunity to begin executing a strategy to correct them—and move forward.

MARKETPLACE LESSONS I'VE LEARNED ALONG THE WAY

What I now know _____

The ever-evolving marketplace is a tough no-nonsense teacher—with real life lessons on execution—whether we are ready to learn—or not.

MARKETPLACE LESSON: Be What You Say

While I was standing in line for a cuppa joe at a well-known coffee joint, I noticed their Store Action Plan displayed on a wall (for anyone to see). The stated goal was "to improve our standing and grow sales by:

1. increasing staffing

2. cleaning and sweeping to improve store cleanliness

3. dynamic development

4. providing flawless execution of promotional platforms."

As I waited (a long time) for my turn, I looked around. One barista was serving the growing line in a store so dirty and grungy my wife refused to stay and drink her coffee there.

We've often been told that by publicly declaring our plan of action we're less likely to stall out or slide backward. We feel committed to carrying through with our plan. Not in this case.

Lesson Learned:

"Owning a plan is a very important step. However nothing happens until the plan is executed." —S.G.

MARKETPLACE LESSON: Give Feedback

When she was 15, my wife became a camp counselor for the first time. At her mid-summer review she was told that her performance was poor. The director very clearly outlined her weaknesses and indicated that improvement was necessary if my wife wished to be hired back the following summer.

At the summer's-end review she was told that her performance had taken a 180 degree turn from the previous month. The director was thrilled and offered her a job for the next year.

After several summers, my wife became the camp's director. To this day she says that, without the straightforward and honest review that she received mid-summer, she would never have realized her shortcomings and worked to improve them.

Lesson Learned:

"It's so necessary to give and receive honest and direct feedback. Once you are aware of your conduct, attitude, performance, it becomes possible to change. (Sometimes you also need to step back and ask some key questions of yourself.)"—S.G.

MARKETPLACE LESSON: Listening Well Is a Big Deal

When we go out to eat my wife always asks for her glass of water without ice. We've kept track. She gets water with ice about 75% of the time. Why? Because most of the time the waiter isn't really listening. Okay, getting the request for a glass of ice water correct (or not) is no big deal. But when "not really listening" is prevalent in more important situations in our business world, it is a big deal.

"Not really listening" causes loss of productivity and therefore loss of profitability, if for no other reason, than the need to re-do something. It causes frustration, bad feelings, misunderstandings. It inhibits business success. Ask around. Are you a good listener? If not—take action to start really listening.

Lesson Learned:

"We were given two ears but only one mouth, because listening is twice as hard to do as talking."—S.G.

MARKETPLACE LESSON: Awareness Precedes Action

A client of mine in the manufacturing business was having a very difficult time controlling waste. He said the specialty stainless-steel screws used in the production process littered the shop floor. He was at a loss about how to get workers to pick up these screws.

One morning he hit on a great idea. During the lunch break, he threw hundreds of nickels on the shop floor. When the workers returned, they eagerly ran around picking up the nickels. He then explained that each screw left on the shop floor was the same as a nickel being left there. The light of understanding finally dawned on the faces of the workers. Action followed.

Lesson Learned:

"Communicate clearly on the level of the listener. One concrete example is worth a thousand abstract words."—S.G.

PART IV:
EXECUTION PARTNERS

Chapter Fifteen: CAPITALIZE ON INTERNAL AND EXTERNAL RESOURCES

What I now know _____

Today no business is an island. We all need resources to enable us to reach our goals—to execute our plans.

Every organization flies or falls by the resources it maintains. Maximizing the value—the capabilities—the uniqueness of your resources assists you to retain a sustainable competitive advantage.

High-performance organizations recognize that, in order to differentiate themselves from their competitors, they need not only to develop resources and capabilities that are difficult to copy, but also to renew and revitalize those resources continuously. They focus their attention on preserving their marketplace advantage by sustaining strategically valuable core competencies.

INTERNAL TANGIBLE RESOURCES

Tangible resources are the talisman for powerhouse retailers like Wal-Mart and Costco. They run their huge operations systems with ultimate precision. Their financial clout is almost impossible to duplicate. Yet every entrepreneur (big or small) can search for and find hard-to-copy ways to improve their own operations. Looking to the big guys for inspiration can be valuable. Manco CEO Jack Kahl, remarked that when his company, which markets a wide variety of professional and consumer adhesives, was a

"When a thing has been said and well, have no scruple. Take it and copy it."

—Anatole France (1844-1924), novelist

young fledgling company he paid particular attention to the strategies of the giants, and copied them whenever he could. (Today Manco itself, is worthy of emulation.)

Other tangible resources that can be garnered to provide powerful differentiation and competitive advantage include research and development, the use of innovative technology and equipment, and corporate infrastructure, to name but a few. Capitalize on your tangible resources. They will provide you with new opportunities for effective execution.

INTERNAL INTANGIBLE RESOURCES

"The ability to learn faster than your competitors may be the only sustainable competitive advantage."

—**Arie De Geus,** former Corporate Planning Director, Royal Dutch Shell

Opportunities for intangible resources abound—a great reputation being one of the most valuable.

Quality and culture and speed are also considered valuable intangible resources that offer powerful and effective differentiation—and an innovative opportunity for execution.

American Apparel doesn't make clothes in Asia, where workers are paid pennies an hour, and then ship them to be sold at rock-bottom prices in the United States. Dov Charney, the founder has a different business model, one that highlights his intangible resource—speed. This has become his competitive advantage. He manufactures in a Los Angeles factory, and then ships the clothes to wholesalers and his company-owned stores (worldwide)—fast. He can get new designs to the shelves in four days, something that would have been impossible, if he had relied on the traditional "Wal-Mart" product model (i.e., contracting factories in Asia to manufacture entire inventories of clothes months ahead of the delivery date).

HUMAN RESOURCES

Manpower is an organization's secret weapon. Human capital must therefore be the starting point of any plan and remain its foundation to ensure successful execution. A competitive advantage in this area can be created by enabling knowledge creation and by building executable learning processes. However, this is easier said then done. It can't be stressed too frequently—employees must be given the tools to perform the new knowledge-intensive tasks required to move their organizations forward.

An Accenture Executive Issues survey, focusing on strengthening an organization's human capital, asked executives to select the staffing issues that weigh most heavily on their minds. The survey's results offer insight for action.

"The hardest customer you have to satisfy are the people who work for you."

—Sam Geist

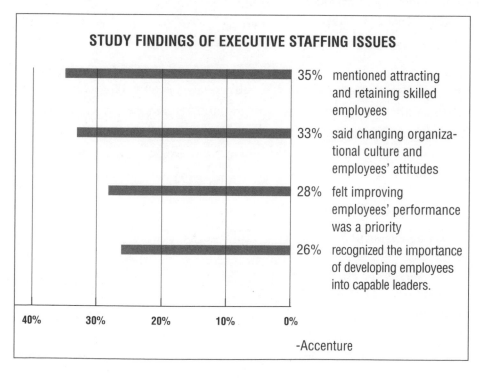

STUDY FINDINGS OF EXECUTIVE STAFFING ISSUES

35% mentioned attracting and retaining skilled employees

33% said changing organizational culture and employees' attitudes

28% felt improving employees' performance was a priority

26% recognized the importance of developing employees into capable leaders.

40%   30%   20%   10%   0%

-Accenture

Operating within an environment that focuses on the strengths of human-resources often requires a change in the mind-set of senior managers. Managers must move from being analytically driven strategy directors to becoming people-oriented strategy mentors. They must utilize a strategic recruitment process that attracts the best of the best. They must nurture individual expertise and initiative, then leverage it by sharing the results across the company. They must provide appropriate training and cross-training to enable their staff to accept the challenges inherent in tomorrow's workplace.

> *"In a company of 60 people with millions of customers and a growth curve like, well like Google, there wasn't room for specialists or walls around a person's role. Your job was whatever the day demanded and if you needed to learn HTML or Swahili to do it, that was your job too."*
>
> —**Doug Edwards** (ex-Googler)

> *"By the end of the decade it is expected that 10 million more jobs will be available than workers to fill them."*
>
> —**U.S. Bureau of Labor Statistics (2006)**

Today's organizations do not merely compete for product markets or technical expertise. They compete for the commitment of their staff. After persuading them to join their organization, management must ensure that those valuable individuals become connected to the organization through ongoing learning and remain deeply connected to the company's ideals and aspirations. This bonding process also requires that staff acquire a sense of achievement from executing the strategy—and ever move forward.

EXTERNAL RESOURCES

> *"More and more of us are faced with having to achieve breakthrough goals and to solve complex problems. You can't do that alone. The only way to meet these kinds of challenges is through collaboration."*
>
> —**Robert Hargrove,** executive business coach and consultant, author

At the same time, high-performance organizations realize they can't go it alone. They need partners to help them move their plans, and strategies to execution.

Choose wisely, since your partner's capability, efficiency, service and culture strongly reflects on your organization. When your shipment of fresh turkeys for Thanksgiving doesn't arrive as promised, your customers aren't upset with your distribution channel because of a double-booked truck; they're upset with you.

YOUR DISTRIBUTION CHANNEL RESOURCE

Controlling the flow of goods and services from their point of origin to the point of consumption (especially worldwide) is almost impossible to accomplish without professional logistical support. Logistics has become an indispensable tool in business today as it integrates information, transportation, inventory, warehousing, handling and packaging.

A major component of logistics for many marketers is the specific distribution activities that take place in order to ensure that their products are available to their customers when and where they need them. Monitoring and managing the distribution channel that proves to be most effective for you is at once essential for high-performance and vital to moving your organization forward.

While there are many avenues open to them for distribution, John Deere sells its tractors through both its dealer network (3,200 dealers across the United States) as well as through The Home Depot. (The Home Depot sells only the entry-level 100 series—and is linked to a local dealer who carries out servicing and a pre-sales inspection.) Online you can buy certain tractors directly from John Deere—but they are all delivered and serviced by a local dealer, because John Deere wanted to keep them in the loop.

The benefits of this distribution channel are four-fold—: the pre-sales inspection by a competent dealer mechanic has cut the return rate to low single digits for tractors purchased at The Home Depot; dealers have benefited with extra sales from customers who wanted to buy more powerful models. Dealers are also able to follow-up with customers after the purchase, and they are paid for every machine they set up for The Home Depot; consumers (especially women) feel comfortable buying a brand name from a reputable dealer, so sales increase; John Deere, now in the mass market, continues to be a reputable and powerful brand name a century after it began.

By conducting customer research, listening to feedback, and satisfying all partners in the distribution channel, John Deere is able to successfully execute its plan.

YOUR OUTSOURCING RESOURCE

> *"It was difficult for us to let go of some of the control, but we realized that we had to—if we wanted to continue to grow the business."*
>
> —**Kimberly Fox,** founding partner, Upstart Communications

Outsourcing became popular in the 1980s, and has grown exponentially in our globalized environment. It is often used to lower company costs, to utilize external competencies, or to take advantage of external technologies or resources. Once again, it is vital to match your organization's quality and service-level expectations, culture, integrity, and specific product requirements with those of the company to whom you have outsourced. Even though you may feel you have given away a part of your organization's competency, you must remain integrally involved in the process.

ICI (one of the world's major coatings, adhesives, starch and synthetic polymers businesses) has outlined its expectations for its business partners loud and clear, for all to read on the Internet. ICI's specific requirements begin with the expectations that partners (including suppliers) will operate with values similar to its own. Of particular concern to ICI are—: business integrity, employee responsibility, environmental stewardship, and customer and supply-chain responsibilities.

ICI also clearly states that the repercussions of failing to adhere to the values outlined "will lead us to take corrective measures which could lead to termination of our business relationship." No leeway! No surprises! A long-established reputation is at risk!

Effective use of outsourcing, no matter if it is for products or services can strengthen weaker core competencies as well as provide a productive and profitable competitive advantage. It is also able to pave the way for effective execution of the strategy.

THIRD PARTY RESOURCES

Consultants are often-used external resources. Their role can vary from being an extra pair of hands, or an expert in the situation, to being a collaborative partner.

From marketing plans to technology issues to financial management to employee recruitment to fundraising planning to strategic planning—are all within the capabilities of the right consultant. Their objective third party perspective on the situation is a definite advantage.

I have often been asked to come into an organization for just this reason—to provide an unbiased outside perspective and offer up suggestions for improvement—for change. I have found that staff members are frequently more willing to speak up and relate concerns to a third party when "the boss" is not directly involved.

Often solutions that become quite apparent to an objective observer (but not to those so immediately involved) are quite easily incorporated into the execution strategy—enabling the organization to move forward.

ALTERNATIVE RESOURCES

Small businesses that might find the costs of an independent consultant prohibitive have other resources available to them—: Chambers of Commerce, Boards of Trade and small business associations. These organizations are valuable resources, funds of ideas, networking opportunities, education, regulatory information, and more. Often their programs, conferences and lectures provide an opportunity to discover new perspectives that will assist you to better execute your strategy.

Executing your ideas, your strategies grows out of utilizing the resources to be found within your organization as well as those capabilities you import as part of your external-resources strategy. By maximizing all of these competencies your organization moves to the front of the class.

RATE YOURSELF

On a scale of 1 to 10: How well does my organization use its internal and external resources to execute its strategy?

What can be done to improve the utilization of these resources by one point?

_____

_____

_____

_____

THE BOTTOM LINE

Internal and external resources have the capability of expanding the reach of your business—if you choose and use them wisely.

Chapter Sixteen: MASTER TECHNOLOGY

What I now know _____

Technology is transforming our private lives—and our business lives whether we know it or not—whether we understand it or not—whether we like it or not.

As technology sweeps across the globe, it changes everything in its wake—including the way our society operates and the way our businesses run. Technology is now inextricably connected to your business, providing a vehicle to differentiate yourself. It's an accelerator—the fuel we use to speed up the pace with which we create business value. It's an enabler—the information and processes we use to execute our vision, our ideas, plans and strategies.

> *"We're in the middle of a 20-year march. We're just halfway there in terms of realizing the full potential of digital technologies to transform industry and commerce... those who stay focused on innovative applications of new technologies to solve business problems will win big."*
>
> **—Tom Pike,** global managing partner for growth and strategy, Accenture

THE INTERNET

One of the most significant catalysts in the technology revolution is the Internet. It has had a huge impact on the way business operates. It has made small players into big players. The Internet touches everything; everything touches the Internet—leaving us nowhere to hide. The Web is now used to buy, to sell, to find partners, to disseminate information, to communicate... It has enabled e-business to flourish on a global scale. It has heralded the death of distance.

Online arms connected to stores like The Pottery Barn, Crate and Barrel, and Williams Sonoma serve to expand their bricks-and-mortar markets, while cyberstores like Zappos and Amazon, with their free shipping, huge selections and quick turnaround time are very real competitors to traditional marketers. Statistics from a recent Forrester research study indicate that online sales rose 25% to $219.9 billion in 2006 and now comprise 7% of all sales in the United States.

> *"The number one benefit of information technology is that it empowers people to do what they want to do. It lets people be creative. It lets people be productive. It lets people learn things they didn't think they could learn before and so in a sense it is all about potential."*
>
> **—Steven Ballmer,** CEO, Microsoft

Technology has created a cyberworld that mirrors, in detail, our own. In fact, it is very often more accessible, and larger than the real world we know. However like our real world, it is not without problems. Even if we are not interested in living there, we have no real alternative but to do so for a large part of our day.

TECHNOBUSINESS

Information technology and business have converged. The result is a union that combines relevant services to provide customers with a wider set of solutions. Technology has enabled far-reaching connectivity. ExxonMobil now operates completely wired in 240 countries—in 24 time zones. Its interconnectivity has no bounds.

> *"Information technology and business are becoming inextricably interwoven. I don't think anybody can talk meaningfully about one without talking about the other."*
>
> **—Bill Gates,** Chairman, Microsoft

Companies are increasingly choosing to compete by amalgamating their services with complementary businesses. For example, FedEx purchased Kinko's, expanding its capabilities to include the printing and shipping of any document, anytime, anywhere—on time. Determine how you can use technology to expand your capabilities.

Statistics indicate that nearly 50% of all current U.S. capital outlays are IT-related. Technology, in a very real sense, powers your business, and with it IT risks become business risks and IT opportunities become business opportunities.

GLOBAL COMPETITION

While technology has enabled competition to go global, global competition requires improved technology, more efficient operations, and more innovative thinking to fulfill the heightened need for flexibility and speed that is the result.

While in Asia, I saw "speed" first hand. In the commercial harbor of Taipei, Taiwan, huge flatbeds, bursting with hundreds of containers of raw materials, were being offloaded from one side, while hundreds of containers (with goods for export) were being onloaded from the other side.

On the global scene, size matters. The giants see smaller companies as more agile, responsive and closer to customers. They feel smaller companies have the advantage of flexibility. Meanwhile smaller, regional companies envy the power they see wielded by global giants that give global service more easily.

Globalization is rewriting the rules by which companies play by often making it tougher to compete. New technologies and product innovation, although advantageous in the long-term, are also initially challenging, since they must be learned and applied effectively. Open markets force down the price of goods, which is good for the customer but challenging for the provider. At the same time, customers now expect (and often demand) quick turnaround, constant access, and customized solutions—which technology has enabled. Unfortunately demands such as these, as well as the need not only to make faster decisions but to execute them faster, are difficult for organizations (especially large ones) to deliver since they are not accustomed to such speed. Each of us must ask ourselves, where do I find myself in the global marketplace? How am I maximizing my position?

TECHNOLOGY ENABLES OUTSOURCING

Whether you choose to embrace the outsourcing movement or not, you must acknowledge that it exists. Initiated by companies in the United States to enable them to compete with global competitors, outsourcing is now widely a reality of business life—utilized in a wide variety of business sectors from manufacturing to customer service call lines. Recognizing that outsourcing has become a part of the global landscape reminds us that we must execute our strategy with this reality in mind.

TECHNOLOGY ENABLES PRODUCT INNOVATION AND DEVELOPMENT

"The first rule of any technology used in a business is that automation applied to an efficient operation will magnify the efficiency. The second is that automation applied to an inefficient operation will magnify the inefficiency."

—**Bill Gates**, Chairman, Microsoft

Products have always been developed to support the business plan, in order to provide customers with what the marketer thinks they want and need. In today's marketplace not only must those products be commercially feasible, they must also be technically viable. Microsoft has taken its place as a world leader in designing technology that enables its customers (and their customers) to execute—faster and more accurately.

TECHNOLOGY ENABLES SUPPLY CHAIN MANAGEMENT

The most significant advance in supply chain management and logistics technology for the foreseeable future is likely to be radio frequency identification (RFID). Wal-Mart is promoting this new tracking and identification system—as are retailers such as Tesco, Marks & Spencer and Metro Group in the United Kingdom and Germany. U.S. retailers like

Kroger (grocery chain) are also following Wal-Mart's lead. By attaching RFID tags to boxes and pallets, the manual scanning of bar codes of incoming goods is eliminated, resulting in huge savings in labor costs. RFID can also solve retail's two biggest problems—: out-of-stock items and shrinkage. The possibilities of RFID are mindboggling. Technology is becoming the backbone of business. Technology is creating impetus for execution.

TECHNOLOGY ENABLES EVOLUTION

Technology plays a huge role in Amazon's success. Without its capabilities we would not have seen Amazon execute its order-to-delivery process with such speed, accuracy, and efficiency. So valuable is Amazon's innovative process that it now leases out its capabilities to other companies. Amazon has been able to leverage its infrastructure and diversify to such an extent, that it is sometimes referred to as the Wal-Mart of e-commerce. Technology leading execution.

High-end cars like Lexus have installed driver-recognition software. When the driver opens the door, it triggers automatic driver-specific adjustments to seat, temperature, steering wheel and mirrors. This comfortable customization and luxury selling feature are technology-enabled.

TECHNOLOGY IMPROVES PRODUCTIVITY

Retailers are looking to technology to improve their business processes. Fifty-six per cent of retailers polled replied that in the last year their most effective way to improve productivity was to boost their network's bandwidth performance—enabling them to handle a huge amount of product and sales data quickly. This information assisted them make better decisions—which resulted in more sales. Technology leading execution on the sales floor.

Failing to react quickly enough to changes or challenges in the marketplace is risky. Collecting data, analyzing market changes, adapting to consumer trends and making the right decisions are all important for enhanced productivity. To assist marketing staff at Shanghai General Motors Co. Ltd., to speed up their decision-making and IT management, they were given wireless-enabled notebooks. They were then able to connect to the network wirelessly and securely—and act on the information quickly.

Lingerie retailer, Victoria's Secret increased the number of returns it is able to process from 180 to 600 an hour by using scanning technology. Such technology has also greatly reduced the number of errors made by the data-entry staff. At the same time, the large Mid-west law firm of Cruz, Kronis and Koonz increased its productivity by using the Blackberry and Onset Technology to improve customer service, and enable attachment reading, data access and online billing.

No matter where in the marketplace it is used, technology is capable of greatly increasing productivity and profitability when strategic thinking about technology is moved to strategic execution.

TECHNOLOGY ENABLES FORECASTING AND RESPONSE TO CUSTOMERS

Time is the currency of this decade. When new technology enables the instant response that customers demand, it increases a business' value. From customers of products like digital cameras and Linksys wireless routers to those of services like pizza delivery and credit-card swipe n' go, the cry is heard loud and clear—: faster, cheaper, better.

Retailers in the United Kingdom are responding to the need for improved efficiency with the use of new technology. EPOS (electronic point of sale) provides data on business performance by individual sale. It can help pull product information or check stock availability or be integrated with the supply chain, allowing for faster replenishment for companies like DIY chain Wickes. Supermarket giant Tesco launched electronic shelf-edge labeling, which facilitates instant price updates. It also provides accurate pricing in clear displays—and helps customers decide quickly and easily.

TECHNOLOGY FORGES ALLIANCES

Business collaboration unites the efficiencies of two or more companies, enabling them to offer their customers even more than they could alone. Intuit, the developers of QuickBooks, were ready to partner with best-in-class companies to help solve important customer problems.

They chose Google Inc. with which to form a strategic alliance. This alliance helped millions of small businesses promote themselves online, using a variety of popular Google services, that were built into most QuickBooks 2007 products. Many, many other companies have also merged, acquired and formed alliances in order to maximize their efficiencies, and execute productively.

> *"In this new wave of technology, you can't do it all yourself, you have to form alliances."*
>
> —**Carlos Slim Helú**, businessman

TECHNOLOGY ENABLES SOCIAL NETWORKING

Social networking is a current phenomenon of huge proportions. Sites such as Facebook and MySpace have grown exponentially since their creation. As a social mechanism they connect people with common affiliations, enabling them to network with one another. It is through social networks that knowledge is shared, so while on the surface these sites are social, they certainly have workplace implications.

There are conferences being held globally that focus entirely on the value and development of these networks. Recently the success of YouTube and other video-sharing platforms seem to have inspired TeacherTube, a video-sharing site for instructional videos. Its mandate is to provide videos for professional development—teachers teaching teachers. Teachers can post videos designed to be viewed by those interested to learn a concept or a skill. This is technology bringing together social networks and knowledge management—for effective strategy execution.

TECHNOLOGY REWARDS RISK

Although early adopters take greater risks they also collect greater rewards. In today's technologically advanced environment, you must weigh the balance carefully between becoming a risk-taker or not.

Airborne, an air delivery service chose to focus on what it did well, rather than take a risk and use technology to enhance its capabilities. Airborne's conservatism cost it the game. And eventually it was bought by DHL and absorbed by them.

FedEx and UPS on the other hand, took early risks to invest in technology that gave them a huge advantage over competitors like Airborne and enabled them to cross the chasm that later adopters would have difficulty crossing. Their risk in technology has paid off handsomely. They now execute their strategy around the world.

TECHNOLOGY PROVIDES SAFE-STORAGE

In order to keep a company operational, its technology must be safeguarded, since it is not infallible. Because it is so completely integrated with today's businesses, the benefits of technology must be taken seriously—very seriously. Ensure valuable information isn't lost by using a reputable storage and replication system. Business continuity solutions have been available to large companies for years. IBM has provided them with data replication services to ensure continued operations, during "down times."

Companies like Geminare, a focused business continuity partner, realizing the importance of these highly sophisticated techniques to all companies have made them available to small and mid-sized markets, at affordable costs.

Geminare developed and provides a complete turn key business continuity solution to this traditionally under-serviced market, giving SMEs the capability to keep their websites, email, data, and employees working, just like the Fortune 100 companies do.

In this important area new technology and available services have become a great equalizer of big and small.

Maximize the positive impact technology has on your business, by integrating the technology into your execution process.

"Technology happens, it's not good, it's not bad. Is steel good or bad?"

—**Andrew Grove,** founder, Intel Corporation

——— ✳ ✳ ✳ ———

RATE YOURSELF

☐   On a scale of 1 to 10: How well does my organization leverage technology to execute better business outcomes?

What one thing can be done to improve our use of technology by one rating point?

_____

_____

_____

_____

THE BOTTOM LINE

Technology is affecting every aspect of our business lives. Know it well. Understand it well. Use it well. Become the master of technology, rather than letting it become your master, so you are better able to execute your corporate strategy.

MARKETPLACE LESSONS I'VE LEARNED ALONG THE WAY

What I now know _____

*The ever-evolving marketplace is a tough no-nonsense teacher—
with real life lessons on execution—whether we are ready to
learn—or not.*

MARKETPLACE LESSON: The Power of Technology

Nordstrom has always provided the retail marketplace with a lesson in execution. Last night it provided me with a lesson in the power of technology. I went online to get a Nordstrom's gift certificate for my daughter. The denomination I wanted to send was not available from the automated choices. It was late. I was going to give up, when I noticed the "Need Help? Live Chat" button.

I pressed. I was able to send a text message to a "live" customer service rep who was "standing by to provide immediate real time assistance." We chatted back and forth using our keyboards. I explained my problem, she offered solutions. Without any hassle I was able to get the gift certificate for the amount I wanted.

Lesson Learned:

"Technology is a business enabler. Those who provide customer solutions, across a variety of platforms—get the business."—S.G.

MARKETPLACE LESSON: Children Live in Cyberspace

If Webkinz were only fluffy stuffies, kids would probably have relegated them to a shelf in the closet after a few hugs. But they're not. They're fluffy stuffed animals with coded ID tags that allow the owner (my grandchildren) to access the "Webkinz World" website. Here the owners "adopt" a virtual version of their pet and create a home for it—feed it—and take care of it.

This site **http://www.webkinz.com** has so much "real life" stuff going on that parents are instructed by their children to care for their Webkinz when their kids are away. The brainchild of the Ganz toy company, Webkinz have hooked kids to the tune of two million sold and one million users registered on the site—so far.

Lesson Learned:

"Technology has created a cyberworld—a huge profitable world—ask any kid."—S.G.

MARKETPLACE LESSON: The Blog As Marketing Strategy

The recent blog I was forwarded from my son, Michael strongly reminded me of its huge and growing influence. Millions of people write them. Many millions of people read them, comment on them and pass them on.

This blog was about Zappos, a large online shoe store. The writer had ordered seven pairs of shoes from Zappos for her mom who was very ill. Only two fit. The rest were waiting to be returned but because of various circumstances—the shoes were never sent back. There's a 15 day time limit on the returns. Zappos pays the shipping, but you have to get the shoes to UPS yourself.

When she came home this last time, she had an email from Zappos asking about the shoes, since they hadn't received them, so she replied that her mom had died but that she'd send the shoes as soon as she could. They emailed back that they had arranged with UPS to pick up the shoes, so she wouldn't have to take the time to do it herself. That's not their corporate policy.

In her own words: "Yesterday, when I came home from town, a florist delivery man was just leaving. It was a beautiful arrangement in a basket with white lilies and roses and carnations. Big and lush and fragrant. I opened the card, and it was from Zappos. I burst into tears. I'm a sucker for kindness, and if that isn't one of the nicest things I've ever had happen to me, I don't know what is. So...

IF YOU BUY SHOES ONLINE, GET THEM FROM ZAPPOS.

With hearts like theirs, you know they're good to do business with."

Lesson Learned:

"A blog can become a very effective component of your communications program—when executed well."—S.G.

PART V:
THE EXECUTION EXPERIENCE

Chapter Seventeen: EXECUTE FOR YOUR CUSTOMERS

What I now know _____

A business without customers... isn't.

What is the lifetime value of a customer? It's so huge that you must execute as well as you can, so as not to lose a single one of them.

A recent Harvard Business Review study has shown that, on average, an organization loses 50% of its customers every five years—and the price tag for finding new customers to replace the ones that got away is six to seven times the cost of getting them in the first place. Very often efforts to win customers back come to naught. A Gartner Group study reaffirms this finding, stating that 55% of such initiatives to win customers back, fail.

> *"American Airlines calculated that if they had one more customer on each flight in a given year, the difference in revenue would have been about $114 million. How much is one customer worth to you?"*
>
> **—Guerilla Marketing newsletter**

Other studies, including the one conducted by Towergroup, a financial services research and advisory firm, has found encouragingly enough, that as little as a 5% increase in customer retention can boost profits by at least 20% (and as much as 80%, as mentioned earlier in previous statistics), in many businesses. It has also been documented that loyal, repeat customers spend on average about 67% more than new customers. Loyal customers also refer new customers (as many as seven of them) to the business by the time they themselves have made ten purchases.

It is interesting to note that, in light of all this research data, many businesses still only spend 20% of their budget on retaining those valuable existing customer relationships, while 80% of their revenue actually comes from them.

Based on statistics such as these it makes good sense to focus your execution strategy and your budget on providing the customer service that will retain your customers.

INFLUENCING CUSTOMER LOYALTY

1. Know Your Customers

Get to know them intimately. Their wants, their needs, what issues are of concern to them, what they value, what turns them on, what turns them off. (Although the importance of understanding your customers has been discussed throughout the book, it can't be stressed too emphatically.)

> *"If you don't think you need customers, try doing without them for 30 days."*
>
> —**Richard Feinberg**, Director of the Center for Customer-Driven Quality, Purdue University

CustomerTHINK's 2004 survey on "Why Customers Leave" graphically illustrates the importance of knowing what customers value, what customers think, what customers want. It also clearly highlights that many businesses really have no idea what their (former) customers are thinking. Too often companies and their customers are not on the same wavelength which makes effective execution next to impossible.

One way to get to know your customers better is to talk to them—really talk to them when they're in your store, when they're using (or considering) your service, when they're buying (or considering) your product. Ask them questions, let them talk and talk and talk, while you listen and listen and listen. (In this case listening *is* executing.) Find out what their highest needs are. (Ask yourself, how close are you to addressing their highest needs?)

Companies like Wal-Mart, GE, Starbucks, and Hewlett-Packard, to name just a few, have realized that today's customers want the companies

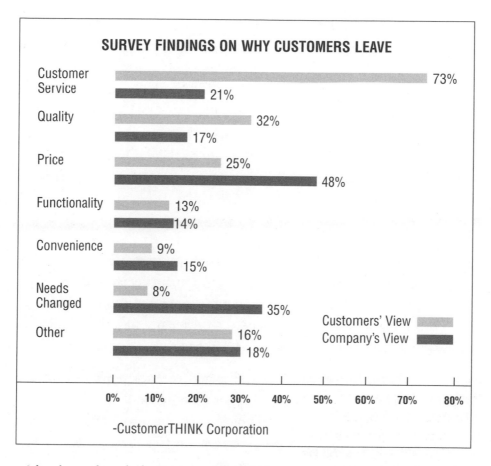

with whom they do business to be good corporate citizens. They have discovered that it pays to take actions that not only benefit their customers but also their customers' environment—the larger society. And they're doing it by advocating "green" solutions, recycling, buying "fair trade" coffee, promoting fluorescent bulbs, and so on. With so much research available today, with so many customer-oriented studies there really is no excuse for not knowing your customers intimately. Shadow them. Go to the places they go, see what they see, read what they read, walk where they walk. Then when you execute you'll do it with their concerns, values and needs top of mind.

> *"Good is not good when better is expected."*
>
> —**Thomas Fuller** (1608-1661), rector of Aldwinkle St. Peter's, Northamptonshire

Before Toyota introduced its new pick-up truck, researchers went to the heart of Texas, the #1 market in North America for pick-up trucks, where they conducted informal investigation. They got to know the people who live there. They observed what Texans were driving—where they were going. They asked what pick-up truck features were important to them. Once they felt they really knew their customers, and their wants and needs, they began to design the Toyota Tundra.

2. Collect Customer Feedback

I stayed at Le Parker Meridien Hotel in New York one weekend and was very surprised by the pre-and-post-stay questionnaires emailed to me. They seemed genuinely anxious to ensure that the room and the amenities they were providing were what I was expecting. After my stay, they wanted to know my thoughts on the experience I had had there.

> *"Do make certain that your customers wants are truly that—and not merely what some people in the company think the customers want. The need for solid customer information is absolute; it will directly affect the quality of everything else that occurs in the process. Garbage in, garbage out."*
>
> —**William Barnard** and **Thomas Wallace**, authors, *The Innovation Edge*

Collecting feedback provides an excellent opportunity to find out what is good and not-so-good about your organization. It has, however, one (significant) caveat. If you ask and you find out, you are really obligated to initiate change—at the very least to ask for more information directly. Not acknowledging the information you have requested is probably worse than not having asked in the first place. (Remember the cruise questionnaire story earlier.)

As outlined in Chapter 14 (pages 106–107), Enterprise Rent-A-Car not only collected feedback but moved the information the company received to introduce strategies that would provide its customers with experiences they would want to repeat. While the questionnaires provided a very useful start to implementation, Enterprise found that talking to customers one-on-one increased customer loyalty exponentially.

Customers in general are very happy to talk about their experiences with your bank, your supermarket, your window-washing service, your car repair, your cleaners, your... Gather the information, determine implementation solutions, put together an execution plan, and begin to execute.

3. Exchange Information with Customers

Having knowledge is not enough. A great customer experience requires that an exchange of knowledge takes place. Think back. Most of our negative experiences as customers occur when the company we are dealing with is unable to give us—as individuals—the answers we want.

Consequences of such experiences go beyond being unpleasant. Research indicates that 80% of buyers stop doing business with a company because of a bad experience. Twenty per cent of those buyers will never do business with the offending company again. Don't get caught in the "overpromising and underdelivering" syndrome. Today customers expect you to honor your promises. They expect more than just good products or low prices. They expect satisfying experiences.

- Have at your fingertips basic product and service information. Have easy access to more detailed information. You can't give information unless you have some to give.

- Build information management directly into the business processes to keep it accurate and up-to-date.

- Facilitate access to information for everyone involved—frontline employees, managers, customers, partners. Share it quickly; no one wants to be kept waiting. Share it across many channels (phone, email, the Web, fax, in person) so it is available at any given time.

Take care that the information isn't altered as it moves across channels, since this would lead to confusion. Maintaining a common information foundation across the company ensures accuracy and reduces the total cost of information management.

- Utilize self-service where it is most effective.

Self-service can be delivered via the Web and automated voice. On the Web, make it as easy as possible for customers to find the information they want with as few mouse clicks as possible. Whenever feasible give customers secure access to data from backend systems so they can check orders, track shipments, verify account balances, reset passwords.... Giving information is taking action. Exchanging information enables continuous execution.

4. Use Customer-Focused Culture to Compete for Customer's Loyalty

Companies that maintain a customer-oriented culture have a distinct advantage. ISR, an international employee research and consulting firm, has confirmed that it has found a link between employees' attitudes, a strong customer-driven culture, and execution. ISR espouses the idea that satisfied and committed employees create satisfied customers, because their performance reflects their satisfaction.

> *"Customers do not buy products or services so much as they buy expectations."*
>
> —**Theodore Levitt** (1925-2006),
> American economist and professor,
> *The Marketing Imagination*

5. Add Value from the Customer's Experience

Many companies define value-added from their own perspective. However I have, over the years, discovered that value is defined by the recipient not the provider. It is rooted in your customers' needs.

Successful companies recognize that it is their customers' value-orientation that should direct their strategy and their execution of that strategy. It is easy to recall examples like Starbucks remembering the value customers put on small extravagances; like Apple remembering the value customers put on both the technologically advanced capabilities and the prestige of owning its iPhone (one million were sold its first week on the market); like Westin Hotels remembering the value customers put on sleeping on the sumptuous and stylish Heavenly Bed (now sold in Nordstrom and copied everywhere).

It is also worth mentioning how smaller companies can execute a customer value-orientation. Tawfic Mowaswes is a Guardian pharmacist who treats his customers as if they were friends coming to his home. He always takes time to chat. Whenever I come into his pharmacy he asks how I am, and how my family is. He reminds me of an old-time pharmacist.

My wife had had a hard day and came in with a prescription to be filled and a headache. Before he filled her prescription, he got her a chair, a Tylenol and a glass of water. She's never forgotten his kindness and repays it by being a loyal customer.

Create a customer-oriented culture from both your own perspective, and that of your organization. Demonstrate your customer-oriented culture in the execution of that perspective. Your customers will love you for it and you'll have the profits to show for it.

RATE YOURSELF

☐ On a scale of 1 to 10: How high would your customers rate your organization as a "top-choice-to-do-business-with" organization?

What can your organization do to improve this rating by one point?

_____

_____

_____

_____

THE BOTTOM LINE

We all need customers. To keep them, we must satisfy them, we must delight them, we must execute with them firmly in mind.

MARKETPLACE LESSONS I'VE LEARNED ALONG THE WAY

What I now know _____

The ever-evolving marketplace is a tough no-nonsense teacher—with real life lessons on execution—whether we are ready to learn—or not.

MARKETPLACE LESSON: Deliver More Than Expected

Blockbuster has been renting movies for more than 20 years. Their original business model was simple. They stocked convenient locations with a large selection of videos. Their customers came to the store—rented the videos—took them home—watched them—and brought them back a couple of days later. Blockbuster did well. They were a leader in video rentals. They gave customers what they wanted.

Then along came Netflix, an on-line DVD rental service with more than 65,000 titles offering flat-rate rental-by-mail. Unheard of!

They blew Blockbuster out of the water. So Blockbuster initiated an emergency rethinking of strategy, and geared up to execute.

Yes, now Blockbuster also offers an on-line service, but they're still playing catch up.

Note: This is not the end of the story—now both Blockbuster and Netflix are suffering from the customers' ability to download movies from the Internet directly to their computer or iPod.

Lesson Learned:

"Giving customers what they want is ordinary. Giving customers what they never knew they wanted is extraordinary." —S.G.

MARKETPLACE LESSON: Make Experiences Memorable

On a beautiful sunny Saturday morning a few weeks ago, I went fruit-picking with one of my sons and his family. The pick-your-own-fruit orchard on the outskirts of Boston charged a $10-per-person entry fee and $1.50 per pound for all the fruit you picked—and did we pick! Our adventure cost well over $100.

Hundreds of other families had the same idea. The place was filled with happy families having a great time. This farm that included family fun in their business strategy and then executed it deliciously, enabled us to enjoy a most memorable experience. That was foremost in our minds, not the cost.

Lesson Learned:

"Consumers want special experiences. Provide them, and they are willing to return again and again and pay handsomely to do so." —S.G.

MARKETPLACE LESSON: Satisfied Customers Return

In late December 2006 after a Southwest airplane backed away from the gate, passengers were told the plane needed to be de-iced. Two and a half hours later the plane was good to go, but by then the pilot had reached his hour limit set by the FAA. A new pilot was required. By the time he arrived the plane needed another de-icing. Five hours after its scheduled departure time, the flight was finally ready for takeoff. A customer service disaster, right?

No it wasn't. The pilot walked the aisle of the plane answering questions and providing updates. Flight attendants relayed news on connecting flights. And a couple of days later, passengers received a letter from Southwest with two free round-trip vouchers for another Southwest flight.

On Southwest's staff there is a person in a high-level position who has the responsibility for coordinating the information sent to the frontlines during major flight disruptions and for sending letters (and often flight vouchers) to customers caught in messy flight situations, even those beyond Southwest's control.

Lesson Learned:

"In the words of Southwest's senior manager of proactive customer service communications, Fred Taylor, 'It's not something we had to do. It's just something we feel our customers deserve.' Taking action to satisfy our customers and make them feel important is a lesson we can all emulate."
—S.G.

MARKETPLACE LESSON: Involve Customers

When the seventh and final title in the Harry Potter series was released, it didn't seem to make a difference whether the book was selling full price or was being discounted. It doesn't take a wizard to know that sales for this volume would be record-breaking. In the first 24 hours, Scholastic Corp., the U.S. publisher, estimated that 8.3 million copies had been sold.

The rationale for the tremendous response is that "it's the grand finale so everyone wanted to see how it would be tied up," according to George Jones, Chief Executive of Borders. His next statement bears remembering, "There are a lot of readers out there who had a stake in this."

Lesson Learned:

"Give them 'a stake' and they will come."—S.G.

Chapter Eighteen: SUMMARY—EXECUTE... OR BE EXECUTED

What I now know _____

It's time to take charge and move strategic thinking to strategic doing. It's time to execute.

In the final analysis it is clear that our biggest business challenge is to close the gap between ideas, plans, strategies, and their execution. We may not need a "best practice," but we all need a better practice. We must clear the obstructions that prevent us from achieving our goals—from executing our vision.

One of the key stumbling blocks to successfully turning hopes into reality is the lack of alignment within the company. In order to "do it," all the organization's divisions must be united when it comes to its objectives, tactics, commitment and vision.

Like any other business activity, the complete ideas-to-execution process needs to be systematically managed with rigor and constant attention. Failing to do so essentially leaves the entire process at risk.

A large client of mine who manufactures stylish home accessories, recognized that a response to the constant change that surrounded the organization and its clients was needed. The president issued a directive to staff in all departments, outlining the state of the business environment. His message then went on to say:

> "We must learn more about what WE do. That means all departments must communicate and understand each other. Today, we will start rotating different associates through different

departments, more or less at random. We cannot have different departments going in different directions and not learning from each other. Get ready to move your desk, and more importantly, your mind. Tell us what you've learned. Give us your suggestions. It won't be easy, you'll be inconvenienced, initially slowed down, miss your neighbor and be angry at management. But it will work. It will lead to great things."

"In our business nothing is permanent and everything must be re-thought and reconsidered. The only constant is change and the best way to predict the future is to invent it."

—**The Limited,** American retailer of contemporary women's apparel

My client realized that his company must capitalize on the changes that are occurring in the marketplace or capsize under them. And true to his promise, his instructions to employees did work. It worked slowly—with the frustrations promised in the directive—but the company got better because it destroyed the silos within its building and then created the changes that enabled it to begin better executing its strategy.

FIVE PRACTICES TO ASSIST YOU TO SUCCESSFULLY EXECUTE YOUR STRATEGY

1. Create an Execution Framework

"Learn from the mistakes of others, you'll never live long enough too make them all yourself."

—**Ralph Waldo Emerson** (1803-1882), essayist and poet

Articulate frequently and clearly what you are trying to achieve. Make certain that everyone in the organization understands the big picture. Reiterate your mission at every opportunity.

Discuss why you aren't yet executing as well as you know you should and what issues need to be addressed to give your strategy a push forward. Ask yourself, is it bad strategy or poor execution?

Identify the one most significant area that must be addressed, and focus your energies on that issue—even though there may be several areas that need attention.

Establish a specific target to close the gap. Describe it in sufficient detail so that your employees will recognize when it has been achieved. Attach a specific deadline for achieving it. Work on it every day for 30 days—and it will become a habit. It will become second nature. Studies have shown when you stick to something for 30 days—it's yours.

2. Unite Your People

Although it has been mentioned previously (and many times) it's worth repeating again. The task at hand requires that your people understand the value of their work and the importance of working together. The era of "silo-thinking" and "silo-working" is long past. It is vital that your people acquire both the skills and the attitude to work toward company goals (and that their own personal goals don't encumber your goals).

3. Build the Environment You Want

Employees learn quickly by example. They see what you are doing. They see how you spend your time. If you build the environment you want by devoting your effort to moving strategy to execution, their effort will follow. Your attitude and your actions

"In the old world you devoted 30% of your attention to building a great service and 70% of your attention to shouting about it... in the new world it inverts."

—**Jeff Bezos,** CEO, Amazon

have the power to unleash the potential and commitment of your employees to assist you achieve your goals.

4. Drive Improvement Forward

Monitor performance frequently, personally, and publicly. This demonstrates that you are paying attention to progress.

Measure the results using a wide variety of indices to get a more rounded picture of the progress that has been made. Analyze the findings to uncover precisely what actions have contributed most to progress. Discover a better practice or three. Then employ these better practices in such a way that they assist in improving performance again and yet again.

"The first responsibility of a leader is to define reality. The last is to say thank you."

—Max DePree, Chairman Emeritus, Herman Miller, Inc., writer

Celebrate achievements, even small ones, so everyone in the organization quickly realizes that their leaders really do care.

Celebrating successes is an undervalued motivator, as I've indicated earlier. So is saying "thank you." Most company leaders don't remember to acknowledge achievement—thereby missing out on an invaluable tool for motivation. Each small achievement not only creates a sense of accomplishment, it raises the bar higher—setting a new benchmark from which to measure further achievements. At the same time it elevates employees' self-esteem and the esteem of their peers.

Report findings. Design the actual reporting to motivate effective action further, by ensuring that everyone knows how well they are doing, how well their team is doing, how well other teams are doing, and that everyone else knows how well they and their team are doing.

Make employee ownership part of the process. Employees who feel that they have made a difference—who feel they are successful in achieving what they have set out to do, are motivated to fly.

Finally, to drive strategy forward to execution, provide employees with what they need to do the job—from tools to information to resources to one-on-one suggestions and advice.

5. Adjust. Change. Improve. Execute

Learn as you go. Adjust the plan along the way based on intermediate results. Fine-tune or change the plan based on your findings. Get better. Implement to improve and grow.

No one will say to you, "Because you did such a good job this year, you can take next year off." This year's efforts and successes become the baseline for next year's accomplishments. In business you are expected to raise the bar and repeat the cycle… again and again.

Train yourself to finish this statement on an ongoing basis: "Business would be better if only…" Ask your people to finish the statement. All your answers will lead you to new perspectives and new opportunities to execute.

Studies have shown that the reason 95% of businesses are not successful is that they are not willing to do what the 5% who are successful are willing to do. Membership in the 5% club requires that the following list of seven achievements are checked off—:

- Operate the business with a sense of purpose. Have a plan of where your business is going. No aimless wandering.

- Engage in open and clear communication. No big secrets. No tall silos. No excluded employees.

- Focus on accountability. Who does what by when. Delegate responsibility. Give authority. Stay in the loop.

- Encourage flexibility and adaptability. Be willing to collaborate for the well-being of the company. Be ready to "zig" when the competition "zags."

  "The trouble with following the herd is stepping in what it leaves behind."

  —the Robertson Stephens Contrarian Fund

- Take a circular approach. Change is continuous. Improvement is continuous. Execution is continuous. No beginning, no end.

- Maintain "a company of leaders" perspective. Learn from everyone in the company. Teach everyone in the company—from top to bottom.

- Use all your resources—internal and external—beneficially. Keep in mind that technology is an invaluable resource today.

"Strategy is a commodity. Execution is an art."

—**Peter F. Drucker** (1909-2005), writer, management consultant and university professor

Innovation, strategies and plans cannot move forward alone. Without execution they lie dormant in a heap. I've always told program participants, "I'll give you a dime for an idea—but I'll give you a dollar if you execute that idea." Execution is everything today. Get your people to execute. Take charge of execution. Move strategic thinking to strategic doing.

At the conclusion of my seminars and workshops I ask participants what was their one take-away—the one idea they will remember and act upon. If time permits everyone shares their take-away. Often I receive emails from participants after the program.

The following are two emails I received recently that I would like to share with you.

Sam,

The seminar was informative. The one comment that hit home as my take-away was "Execution Trumps Strategy". Can't tell you how many times I have been involved with great business plans, however the results always seem to come up short of expectations. Execution and follow-up seem as though they should just happen as the result of a good plan or strategy. Many times the majority of time is spent developing strategies, and then communicated and turned over to the appropriate staff members, then we just wait for the favorable results to flow in. I am going to adjust my time allocation to at least 50/50 with developing strategy / implementation and follow-up. Historically, the time allocation has been probably closer to 80/20.

Thanks. Mike

Dear Sam,

Many thanks for the inspiring paper and the presentation I just received.

I thought of many things to bring home to Denmark, but the most central was the inspiration to act instead of consider.

My phrase came out to be: "Do what I think—instead of think what I do!"

The only way to avoid making mistakes is to avoid taking action. Many thanks, Jakob

What is your take-away from this book now that you've finished reading it? Email me with your comments: **samgeist@geistgroup.com**

I hope a few of the ideas have encouraged you to flatten your forehead—at least slightly. Adapt, alter, maneuver the ideas. Put arms and legs on them—execute them—use them to move your business to the next level.

RATE YOURSELF

☐   On a scale of 1 to 10: How well is my organization executing today?

What can it do to improve its execution by one rating point?

_____

_____

_____

_____

THE BOTTOM LINE

Ideas alone are not enough. Implementation—execution is absolutely mandatory to stay in the game. Execute or Be Executed.

AFTERWORD: ADDITIONAL RESOURCES

During my research and reading for this book I came across some thought-provoking studies and articles on the Internet, that are worthy of note. Since the material is related to the information found in "Execute... or Be Executed," I felt it would provide readers of the book with interesting additional resources.

The titles and descriptions of the materials are outlined below. Direct links to the sites are available on our website at: **http://www.samgeist.com/ executeorbeexecuted/additionalresources**

In the interest of continued learning and execution, I will email, once a calendar quarter, notification of additional reports and information that I have read that may be relevant to you. These links will also be available on our website. Should you wish to receive these quarterly mailings, email to samgeist@geistgroup.com with "quarterly reports" as the subject.

"Six Ways to Make Sure Your Customers Love Your Company"
A discussion of customer satisfaction.

"What Keeps 'Em?"
A report about employee retention and engagement drivers.

"Making the Workplace Work Better"
A survey of the employee landscape.

"I Quit... But Forgot to Tell You!"
An article on the disengaged worker.

"Engaging the Massive Middle"
A report on keeping good people during a talent war.

"Key Insights for the Strategic Leader"
An article on leadership.

"Surviving Disaster: Business Continuity Planning"
An article on the necessity of instituting a business continuity plan.

"Building Competitive Advantage Through People"
An article about capitalizing on human capital.

"Greenbiz.com"
A site about why and how-to become a "green" business.

"The Expanding Digital Universe"
A white paper on Worldwide Information Growth.

"Performance Leadership"
A report on effective business management.

"U.S. Small Business Administrative Resource"
A government website with ideas for small business.

"What Makes The Job So Tough?"
A report on burnout in human services.

"Sharpening Your Business Acumen"
An article on incorporating external trends into internal strategies.

"Executive Issues—High-performance and The Need for Balance"
A survey of top executives to identify top business issues.

"Smart Internet 2010 Report"
A report on the state of the development of the Internet.

"Employment Dynamics and Growth Expectations Report"
A report on the dynamics between employees and employers.

"The Under-Management Epidemic"
A study on disengaged leaders.

"Retention Matters"
A report on turnover and retention of employees.

"Innovation 2005"
A global survey on innovation.

INDEX

ABOUT THE AUTHOR

Sam Geist is a corporate consultant, professional speaker, and facilitator to companies and associations across the globe. He conducts industry-related and company-specific research, in order to prepare and present a variety of customized, actionable programs that focus on business strategy, leadership, customer service, the changing marketplace and maximizing staff productivity.

During seminars, interactive discussions and brainstorming workshops, Sam encourages participants to question themselves, to think about their business in new ways in order to capitalize on their resources, turn their knowledge into action and grow. He insists that asking tough questions—and answering them honestly—is crucial to the well being of every organization.

By each program's end, participants have the tools, know-how, and incentive to turn their ideas into action.

His most requested programs include:

"Why Should Someone Do Business With You…Rather Than Someone Else?"
— strategies to get and keep customers
   (based on his book of the same title)

"Execute…or Be Executed"
— moving strategic thinking to strategic doing
   (based on his book of the same title)

"Look Out! Here Comes Tomorrow"
   — managing change actively

"Would You Work For You?"
– *maximizing leadership ability*
  (based on his book of the same title)

"If I Hear Customer Service One More Time, I'll…"
– *providing exemplary customer service*

"Differentiate…or Die"
– *marketing to maximize competitive advantages*

Sam Geist writes *QuickBites* a weekly e-newsletter which offers subscribers business information for their daily business lives.
Sam Geist can be found online at **www.samgeist.com**

Addington & Wentworth Inc. offers corporate rates on orders of ten or more books.
Please call 1-800-567-1861 or email Sam Geist directly at **samgeist@geistgroup.com** to enquire about volume discounts.